Heart
Monitor
Training

for the

Compleat
Idiot

D1016593

Heart
Monitor
Training

for the

Compleat
Idiot

John L. Parker, Jr.

BREAKAWAY BOOKS
HALCOTTSVILLE, NEW YORK
2009

Heart Monitor Training for the Compleat Idiot
Third Edition
©1993, 1998, 2009 by John L. Parker, Jr.

Published by Breakaway Books
P.O. Box 24
Halcottsville, NY 12438
www.breakawaybooks.com

ISBN: 978-1-891369-84-1

Front cover art by Chris Pyle
Back cover photograph by Rock Nelson
Manufactured in the United States

Library of Congress Cataloging in Publication Data

Parker, Jr., John L., 1947-
Heart Monitor Training for the Compleat Idiot
1. Running--Training. 2. Heart rate monitoring. 3. Physical fitness. I. Title.
796.42'5--dc20
3rd edition Library of Congress Control Number: 2009924620

Printing history

1st printing	April 1998
2nd printing	November 1999
3rd printing	September 2002
4th printing	November 2004
3rd edition first printing:	May 2009
3rd edition second printing	March 2010

Jun 2010

Preface

While this book was written primarily for runners, the principles expressed here apply to cycling, swimming, cross-country skiing, in short, any single-sport endurance training. Multi-sport training and cross-training are a different matter and we deal with them, as well as with non-running sports, in Chapter 16. Athletes interested in multi-sport training are urged to read about the principles of single-sport training first before getting into the much more complex challenge of blending different sports into a coherent training regimen.

Those readers looking to use a heart monitor for general fitness are urged to read Chapter 17 first, then start at the beginning to learn how to best adapt the monitor to their particular exercise activity.

Contents

This book is for my mother, Florence A. Parker . . .

1. A Promise and a Guarantee

Give me a month. Actually two would be better, but one should be enough to prove the point. Putting the simple training theory in this book to practical, day-to-day use will require some self-control—not to push yourself to train harder, but actually to do a lot of your running *easier*.

If, at the end of the month, you're not running, racing, and feeling better than you ever thought possible, send this book back to me, and I'll send you a refund and a certificate of apology suitable for framing.

I'm convinced the approach in this book is absolutely the best way to train for distance running events. I'm also convinced that most people—even some very good runners—do it *wrong*.

So do yourself a giant favor. Stick to this program for a month even if it seems strange or even silly at times. At the end of that time if you're not convinced, go back to what you were doing before —with a refund in your pocket and my humble apology framed on your wall.

If you're skeptical—as you may well be—I urge you to turn to Chapter 11 and read one or two of the actual case studies of runners who have used this method. They tell their stories in their own words, and you'll find their experiences both instructive and inspirational.

Once you realize from their experiences what you can achieve using this method, you'll find it easier to commit to a program that many athletes at first find counterintuitive.

And one more thing. Forget all the cocka-mamie stuff you may have heard or read about using a heart monitor to make sure you're running in your "training zone," and other such folderol—some of which "information" may actually come from the manufacturer of your heart monitor. In my opinion it's an utterly useless way to approach heart monitor training. And it's misleading and will prob-ably leave you more confused about using the tech-nology than you were before you started.

Chapter 2: Out the Door, With a Plan!

L et's get you out the door on your first day of heart monitor training. First we need to establish a working approximation of your Maximum Heart Rate, which is the number of beats your heart produces when it is going all out. You wouldn't happen to know that number off the top of your head, would you? No? Well, don't feel bad. Hardly anyone does.

The standard, so-called scientific way to find your actual Max Heart Rate is to go to a trained professional and get a treadmill stress test for about $150. And because these tests are often administered to cardiac patients, the testers tend to be a little on the conservative side in order to prevent patients from throwing myocardial infarctions right there on the machine. So even after plunking down all that money, you still may not have an accurate number. I've even heard runners say things like "I had a stress test and my Max Heart Rate is 175. But I've seen it at 183 during a race." Hey, Bosco! If you've seen 183, and it wasn't caused by running through a field of microwave towers, your max *is*

Treadmill testing

3

183.

Basically then, I'm not that big a fan of treadmill tests unless they're given by physiologists accustomed to dealing with athletes rather than cardiac patients.

Fortunately, there are some informal ways to find out your actual *physical* Max Heart Rate. You probably get there, for instance, during a short race (one mile to 5K), or possibly during an intense interval workout (e.g., 5 X 220 on the track). If you're going "all out," either of those situations would probably get you to within five beats or so of your maximum. Since all other calculations depend on this number, it really is important to find out what it is. That's why in Chapter 4, we take you through our recommended Max Heart Rate Workout, which is specifically designed to get you to your Max Heart Rate quickly and efficiently (and without spending $150).

Estimating your Max Heart Rate

For the time being, let's use a general age-based formula to get an approximation. We can always adjust it later after you've done the Max Heart Rate workout, or as you become more familiar with your pulse ranges.

Read through the description below, then go to the worksheet area on page 10 and do your own calculations.

The best general formula for athletes[1] is:

205 minus 1/2 your age

The Formula

Example: A 40-year-old male runner:

	205
	−20
Approximate Max Heart Rate	185

Another example: A 28-year-old male runner:

$$205$$
$$\underline{-14}$$

Approximate Max Heart Rate   191

Fudge factors

Based on my experience testing hundreds of runners, I usually add a "fudge factor" of 5 beats each for women and/or for long-time competitive runners. I find that 90% of the time or more, this approach will predict to within a few beats a runner's actual max. (Unfortunately, there is no way to tell whether any individual runner is going to fall outside this predictive curve, so the Actual Max Heart Rate workout is still required to verify the number.)

Recovery Ceiling and Threshold Floor

Once we have either an approximate or actual Max Heart Rate, there are really two numbers we need to calculate to be able to use a heart monitor for effective training. Once we know them, we will post them on the refrigerator, memorize them, tattoo them on our foreheads. These two numbers are the secret key to heart monitor training:

1. Your 70% level, or Recovery Ceiling (by far the more important one) and,

2. Your 85% level, or Threshold Floor

☞   *This is important. The two numbers above, your Recovery Ceiling and your Threshold Floor (and knowing how to use them) constitute 95% of heart monitor training. The rest is just icing on the cake.*

For now, let's get you out the door with a heart monitor on your wrist and a clear idea of what you're trying to accomplish on your first day.

First we need to work out your personal numbers. And let me give you a little reassurance right up front. This may seem to get a little complicated, but believe me, you're not going to have to sit down with a calculator before every workout. Once you've done it this one time, with some possible minor adjustments later, you've pretty much got it.

Here's the formula for figuring your Recovery Ceiling (70% of your Max):

The Recovery Ceiling Formula

(MAX – Resting HR) X .70 + (Resting HR)

What this formula (known as the "Karvonen Method"[2]) does is to figure 70% of your maximum heart rate, but isolates your base Resting Heart Rate from the percentage calculation (since it's as low as your pulse gets, we want to exclude it as a variable). The Resting Heart Rate is added back in after the percentage is calculated. This method tends to give a higher recovery ceiling, but trends closer to the straight percentage curve as it gets higher. (If this doesn't make sense right now, don't worry about it.)

A Sample Case

Example: Let's take our 40-year-old runner, Bob Blaster. We've already calculated that he's got a max heart rate of 185. He wakes up in the morning, and before he even gets out of bed, he takes his pulse to determine his resting pulse. Let's say our runner is in pretty good shape, and his resting pulse turns out to be 45.

Here's how Bob's numbers would look:

(Max Heart Rate – Resting Rate) X 70% + (Resting Rate)

Or: $(185 – 45)$ X .70 + (45)

Which becomes: (140) X .70 + 45

Which further reduces to: 98 + 45

Which gives us a 70% Ceiling of: 143

Bob's projected Recovery Ceiling is 143, which means that if he is scheduled for a recovery day, he should attempt to keep his pulse close to, but *below* 143. (This is by far the most important number to know to effectively use a heart monitor in training.)

The Threshold Floor Formula

Now, let's use the same formula general to determine his 85% level, or Threshold Floor:

(Max Heart Rate - Resting Rate) X 85% + (Resting Rate)

Or: $(185 - 45)$ X $.85 + (45)$

Which becomes: (140) X $.85 + 45$

Which reduces to: $119 + 45$

Which gives us a Threshold Floor of: 164

This runner's projected Threshold Floor is 164, which means that if he is scheduled for hard day, say a tempo run, he should attempt to keep his pulse at 164 or a little above it. If he is doing interval training or speed work, most of the time his heart rate will be even higher.

Apply the Numbers

The Hard/Easy Principle

Now all you need to do is apply these numbers to something you already know: The General All-Purpose Training Principle That Everyone Agrees With But Nobody Follows: Alternate hard days with easy days, better known as the old hard/easy method.

So, if you have worked out your own personal numbers, all you need to decide before you head out the door is: Did I run hard or easy yesterday?

What's that? You say you don't know whether you ran hard or easy yesterday, you just ran?

Well, let me be the first to say: Congratulations! You are truly an excellent candidate for heart monitor training!

The first workout

And let me also say this: for this first workout, let's just assume yesterday was a hard day. This will be true of 90% of the readers of this book anyway. Let's just assume that unless you can swear on a stack of Bibles that you ran so easy yesterday that mothers pushing strollers were zinging by you, call it a hard day.

Work out your numbers first!

Okay, if you haven't already done it, work out your own personal temporary numbers. The worksheet area on page 10 will make it easier. If you don't know what your morning resting pulse rate is, sit back, relax for 60 seconds, take your pulse, then subtract 10 from it. (In Chapter 4 you're going to find out exactly how to get a really accurate Resting Heart Rate.)

All these numbers are approximate anyway, and you'll be adjusting them as you go along. After awhile, the difference of just three or four beats will be very obvious to you, but for now approximations will be good enough.

Before you head out the door for your first recovery run, let me just warn you: If you have an easy time staying under your Recovery Ceiling (Quick: what is your ceiling? 145? 130? 152?), something's probably wrong. Most runners in any kind of shape at all find it all but impossible to stay *under* their ceiling their first few runs.

What if your alarm goes off?

This is particularly true if you have hills on your course, if you get chased by dogs a lot, if you are running with your squeeze, or if you are stressed out from your job with Consolidated Conglomerates Inc. In order to stay under their Recovery Ceiling, some people may even need to do the unthinkable: stop and walk! But just for a few seconds until their pulse comes down.

Well, I'm not going to tell you to lie down and rest every time you hit a hill and you get a beat or two over your ceiling. Use your own judgment. Just try to generally stay below your ceiling for most of your run. Here's a rule of thumb: If you find that you're over your ceiling for more than 30 seconds at a time, *slow down!* Walk if you have to.

Running with "the gang"

And, in case you haven't figured it out already, it's probably not a good idea to do this run with your usual group. They probably run too fast most of the time already, which is exactly what you're trying to avoid. Plus, they're going to laugh at you for your gullibility in trying to use this newfangled gadget to better your sorry self. So do yourself a favor and run with the knuckleheads on your hard day. Let them make all the fun they want. They'll get a big charge out of it right up until the time you start kicking some butts you have never kicked before in races, possibly theirs. Then they'll be sidling up to you and posing polite little queries about heart monitor training. At that point I want you to do me a favor. I want you to tell them about this book. And then refuse to loan them your copy.

Memorize that Ceiling number

So get to it. Quick, what's your Recovery Ceiling? 125? 155? Memorize that number or write it on the back of your hand. If you've figured out how to set up your monitor alarm, go ahead and make that your "upper" range number or as close to it as your monitor will allow (if you haven't mastered the thing yet, don't worry about it).

In any case, get out the door, run one of your usual courses (the least hilly one you can find) and stay under your Recovery Ceiling no matter how embarrassing it seems. See you when you get back.

Recovery Ceiling Worksheet

205

A. Subtract 1/2 your age   −_____

B. Results: _____
   (205 minus A)

C. Add 5 beats if female   _____

D. Add 5 beats if elite   _____

E. Total: (Estimated Max)   _____
   (Add B, C, and D)

F. Minus Your Resting HR   −_____

G. Result: Your "Range"   _____
   (E minus F)

H. Multiply by 70%   X .70

I. Result: _____
   (Range X .70)

J. Add Resting HR back in   +_____
   (Add F back)

Total: Your Recovery Ceiling: _____
   (I plus J)

3. Back from Your First Run: A Quick Evaluation

Okay, you're back. Let's talk about how it went. If you came back from this first run feeling disgusted, ridiculous, humiliated, ready to throw your heart monitor *and* this book into the nearest aerobic goodwill bin, then I say: *Congratulations!* You probably did it right! And don't worry, things are going to get better very quickly.

If you come back with rosy red cheeks, slightly out of breath, feeling as though you really got in a *really good one*, uh, sorry. There's probably something wrong with your math or else your heart monitor is picking up Radio Free Europe.

Ideally, after your first recovery day, you should feel held back, itchy, maybe a little frustrated.

If you're not going to proceed right away to Chapters 4 and 5 to get your Actual Max and Resting Heart Rates, now is the time to make some interim adjustments in your numbers if the first run just felt absolutely *too weird*. For instance, if your ceiling is supposed to be 145, but you found yourself doing even a little huffing and puffing, you need to adjust your Recovery Ceiling downward.

Making temporary adjustments

Try 140 or even 135 next time. A rule of thumb is that at your Recovery Ceiling pace, you should be able to easily carry on a conversation without chopping off sentences to breathe.

Another rule of thumb is the "Two-Minute Rule": Your 70% Recovery Ceiling pace should be about two minutes per mile slower than your 85% pace. That's right. Surprising as it sounds, you can pretty well approximate 70% Ceiling pace by taking your tempo run time on a given course and adding two minutes per mile to the pace. While this generally gives you a very conservative number—probably closer to 65% of Max—it will be very close for most runners.

For example, I have an (approximately) 8-mile trail run I do all the time. My best recent tempo time on the course was 50:14. If I add two minutes per mile, or 16 minutes to that time, I get 66:14. Now, in reality, when I run a true 70% Recovery Ceiling run on the same course, I will time out at anywhere from 61 to 64 minutes, depending on my fitness level at the time. Still, the Two-Minute Rule would get me remarkably close to the correct pace without even using a heart monitor, if I only had the self-discipline to make myself run so slowly!

☞   *Tip: The "Two Minute Rule" can approximate a monitored 70% Recovery Ceiling run by simply adding two minutes per mile to your best tempo run time on the same course.*

Adjusting your Recovery Ceiling the other way—upward—is tricky. Remember, most people will initially find their true 70% Recovery Ceiling pace to be ridiculously easy. That's exactly how an experienced runner should feel during his or her first recovery sessions with a heart monitor.

On the other hand, it is possible for the formu-

The "Two-Minute" Rule

Using the Rule in real life

How to judge the accuracy of your numbers

las to predict way too low in a few individual cases. So if you started going over your ceiling during the first 100 yards, if your monitor started beeping when you tied your shoes, if, in short, you're just absolutely convinced that your temporary Recovery Ceiling should be higher, go ahead and raise it five beats (or ten beats if it seems way off) the next time out.

All this guesswork will go away as soon as you get around to doing the Actual Max Heart Rate workout in Chapter 4. Until then, use your adjusted numbers on your 70% Recovery Ceiling runs.

But let's get one thing absolutely crystal clear: If done correctly, most runners find the first few recovery runs uncomfortably slow. And the better the runner, the more uncomfortable they find it.

If it didn't feel slow, something's wrong

One world class triathlete we know said she felt like wearing a paper bag over her head when she first started running with a monitor, because she didn't want any of her hot shot tri-buddies to see her out training so slow.

But now for the good news: you won't have to go at this tortoise pace forever, even on your recovery days. After several weeks, a miracle begins to happen! You get to go faster, but without violating your sacred Recovery Ceiling!

Egad! What's up with that? Suddenly, life is good, life is sweet. This very pleasant phenomenon is the reward that all good little runners receive if they listen to their heart monitors and stick with the program.

We'll explore physiological underpinnings of this most welcome development in a later chapter. Meanwhile, let's get on with the program.

4. Real Numbers: Measure Your Actual Max Heart Rate

One of the most confusing aspects of using heart monitors in training is the concept of the Maximum Heart Rate. That's unfortunate, because it's the first thing you really need to know to correctly use the device. Once you know how fast your heart will beat when you're going flat out, you can figure out the various percentages you must know in order to design a sensible training regimen.

Your Max Heart Rate doesn't vary much, certainly not as much as your Resting Heart Rate, which goes up and down like a yo-yo, depending on your level of fitness and on a great many other transient variables in your life. But with your Max Heart Rate, after age 30 or so, it remains quite steady from year to year.[1] You may begin to lose a beat or two over the course of a few years, particularly if you're not doing much intense training, but generally speaking, a runner's "max" will remain remarkably constant.

Your Actual Max doesn't vary much

That's the reason I often tell runners that it's easier to determine their Actual Max Heart Rate when they're out of shape. Why? Because as any

Heart Rate monitor user knows, when you're not fit, your Heart Rate skyrockets as soon as you begin to do any training at all, much less anything truly intense. Your Max Heart Rate does *not* go up or down based on your fitness, nor is it higher for great athletes and lower for average ones.[2]

This confuses a lot of people, but it's true. Your Max Heart Rate has nothing to do with ability, nothing to do with fitness.[3] It's a matter of genetics and cardiac efficiency. I've known a former world record holder with a Max Heart Rate under 160 and I've tested an accomplished masters champ who was only a little higher. On the other hand, I've done training runs with average runners who were still able to converse while topping 200!

Your Max isn't a measure of fitness or ability

Another surprising factoid: The standard formulas for approximating Max Heart Rate—like the one we used in Chapter 2 to get you out the door—can be extremely misleading in specific cases. Whether you use the older formula (220 minus your age), or the more refined version (205 minus half your age), whether you build in "fudge factors" as I do, you still may come up with a number that is *way* off[4] (for example, see the box on page 18 with a comparison of my own numbers).

Why the formula max may not be accurate

In any case, determining your Actual Max Heart Rate is the key to constructing a truly scientific heart rate monitor training program. How do you do that? Some physiologists say the only sure way to determine an Actual Max Heart Rate is to do a treadmill test conducted by trained technicians. Yet, as I mentioned in previously, I've known runners who took such a test and (probably because the testers are more accustomed to dealing with cardiac patients and thus are often quite conservative) came away with highly inaccurate results.

Because it is such an important number, I'm often surprised by how confused runners are about their own Max Heart Rate. Runners who say "went over" their "actual max" in a race or a workout are really turned around.

You can't "go over" your actual max

If you see a higher number on your monitor than you thought was your Actual Max, by definition that number becomes your *new* Actual Max, but with this caveat: Watch out for a number that may be an "artifact," i.e. a mistaken output caused by extraneous inputs, such as a nearby TV or radio transmission tower, or another runner's monitor—a very common occurrence—adding in his heart rate to yours, or even some vehicles' ignition systems. My motorcycle, for instance, causes my monitor to go off the scale, and it's not just because I'm scaring myself with my driving. Such artifacts usually produce wild enough readouts that after a little experience with the monitor you will immediately recognize them as bogus. But on the other hand, if you thought your Max Heart Rate was 185, and during an interval workout or a race you occasionally see 187, 192, or even a few beats higher, then you're probably looking at your *new* Actual Max Heart Rate.

Bogus readings from a monitor

One informal method for determining Actual Max Heart Rate is to get a runner to "max out" in a carefully planned track workout.[5] The key in designing such a workout is to get a reasonably well rested athlete's heart working at its highest possible rate before lactic acid build-up or other fatigue factors can begin to inhibit movement and thus give a false low reading. A typical such workout might entail a good warm-up, followed by 4-6 X 400M with a 100M rest jog between each, doing them with increasing intensity, and with the last repeat flat out.

The flat track actual max test

Such tests seem to work fine for some runners, particularly those with track experience, but they can be misleading with others. Many who take up endurance sports later in life, who do not have a background of highly intense intervals or time trials find it difficult to push themselves hard enough on a flat surface to get a true max.

The hill workout method

Doing the same kind of test on a hill, however, is a different story. *Everyone* seems to be able to work up to near max on hills. Consequently, several years ago, after talking with other coaches about this, I finally came up with a simple Max Heart Rate hill workout that, if performed with maximum vigor, will get an athlete to within a beat or two of his or her Actual Max Heart Rate.

Since I have run hundreds of athletes through this test, I'm convinced that if conducted properly it will produce results nearly as accurate—and in some cases *more* accurate—than a treadmill test.

My Own Max HR Numbers below show how far the formulas can be off. I've seen even more extreme examples:

Different formulas give very different results

The Author's Max Numbers Calculated Four Different Ways

Actual (from track test)	Formula A (Sedentary)	Formula B (Fit)
	220	205
	−50	−25
192	**170**	**180**

Actual
(from treadmill
in doctor's office)

185

☞   *WARNING: Of primary concern, of course, is your overall health. Any runner with any question whatsoever about his or her cardiac condition should not do this test until consulting his or her physician. Remember, this test is designed to get your heart beating as fast as it can beat under "normal" circumstances (i.e., without fibrillation), and is thus by definition risky for anyone with any kind of cardiac risk factors. For anyone in that situation, the standard treadmill stress test is by far the preferred method, because if any problems develop during such a test, the personnel and facilities for dealing with it are near at hand.*

The Max Heart Rate Hill Workout

How to do the Max HR hill workout

First, you need to do this test on a day when you are fairly well rested. If you're overly tired from previous training, that may become your the limiting factor rather than your heart's natural max. You don't have to blow a whole workout just to do this test. You can make it part of a longer hill session, or use it as a kind of super-warm-up for intervals or a tempo run. The key is to approach it with reasonably fresh legs and to go at it with the kind of determination you use for an intense interval session or a race. It may seem like a lot of effort just to determine a single rather abstract number, but remember you only have to do it once. The number you get will probably stay the same for many years.

Here is the procedure:

1. Find a fairly steep hill 200-300 meters long.

2. Do the normal warm-up you would do before an interval workout or a race. If you don't

do such a warm-up, horrors! Shame on you. Here's a sample warm-up: two to four very easy miles—at not more than 60-65% of your estimated max—followed by light stretching and some "striders" to get your muscles loose and your heart rate up. (Striders are like 100 meter "wind sprints," except that you accelerate into them for the first 20 meters and de-accelerate the last 20 meters, and run the middle 60 meters at 90 to 95% of your top speed.)

A series of hill repeats will get your heart going

3. Do a series of five repeats up the hill, turning at the top and jogging back down to recover. When you reach the bottom of the hill, you turn immediately and start up on the next repeat. The key is to gradually increase your intensity on each one, so that you're starting each repeat at a higher heart rate than the last. The jog down is your only rest. Check your monitor at the beginning and end of each repeat, and either memorize those numbers or call them out to an assistant to write down for you. It is especially important to keep watching the monitor at the top of each repeat. Your heart rate will usually keep going up for several seconds after you stop, so you must keep watching it until the numbers peak and begin to go back down.

Maxing out on the last repeat

4. On the last repeat, keep increasing your intensity until you are sprinting at least the last 100 yards at your absolute maximum speed. You should finish this last repeat with that totally "blown out" feeling you get from sprinting the last 100 yards of a race, which leaves you gasping for breath and grabbing your knees for support. That's fine, just don't let that keep you from continuing to check your monitor until the numbers start to go back down.

Keep watching that monitor!

5. Keep watching that monitor while you're catching your breath. If you've got a friend helping you, call out the numbers as they increase. Write the number down or get someone to help you

remember it. It's amazing how spacey a runner's mind gets doing a workout like this, so don't go through this whole procedure and get back home only to realize sometime later in the shower that you have no idea what your max number was.

You may hit your max before the last repeat

Note that your Max Heart Rate is the highest number you reach at any point during this workout. You will probably reach your max on the last repeat, but some runners hit it on an earlier one and then get fatigued. At any rate, the highest number you see will probably be as close to your max as you will be able to get.

5. Real Numbers, Part II: Measure Your Morning Resting Heart Rate

This is a considerably less alarming procedure than the max test, and it's one that many athletes do daily, recording the results in their training logs. Although this may seem a bit compulsive, there are some good reasons for doing so.

One is that the general trend lines on your morning resting rate can give you a good overview of your fitness. As you get in better shape, your heart gets more efficient, it pumps more powerfully, with greater stroke volume, and thus your resting pulse gets lower. So low, in fact, that many runners have had the entertaining experience of watching medical personnel get all exercised while taking their pulse or blood pressure. I had one nurse throw away two blood pressure cuffs in a row, claiming that they had leaks. She was wrinkling her brow over the third one when I told her I was a runner, which elicited a sigh of relief and the immediate recycling of the discarded cuffs.

Another reason to take your morning resting

rate at frequent intervals is to alert yourself to other, more transitory phenomena that you may not have otherwise been aware of. You'll certainly be aware that you and Ted Beshakus should never ever have another margarita drinking contest, or that it probably wasn't really worth it to stay up until three in the morning to find out who won the academy award for best supporting hand puppet in a TV miniseries.

But you may not have known that the hard 10-miler you did two days ago took more out of you than you thought. Or that the scratchy throat you felt last night may very well have been turning into something more unpleasant while you slept.

A higher-than-usual morning resting rate can give you advance warning of overtraining or of an oncoming bug, and thus give you that much more time to doctor yourself, back off on training, or to spend more time in bed.

A lower-than-usual pulse can announce the very pleasant news that you're in better shape than you thought you were!

At any rate, although it doesn't have nearly the overall impact as your Max Heart Rate, your Resting Heart Rate is still an integral part of the formulas used to calculate your various percentages of effort, so it's a good idea to get an accurate reading of that number.

In general, runners tend to overestimate their resting heart rate simply because they've never gotten a reading on their heart when it was working at its absolute slowest. Most people have had their pulse taken in the middle of a hectic day, or after they've had a cup of coffee or two, or when they're sitting in the slightly disturbing confines of a medical establishment of some kind, getting ready to undergo some procedure involving a device that looks like a stainless steel Salad Shooter.

What your Resting HR can reveal about your body

That simply won't do.

What we're looking for here, as with the Max Heart Rate, is the absolute lowest heart rate your heart beats at under "normal" conditions, i.e., absent drugs or an abnormal medical condition.

The Procedure

How to find your Actual Resting HR

The time to do this is first thing in the morning, preferably after a restful night's sleep. Keep your monitor and chest strap on your bedside table. (No, it's not necessary—or even advisable—to wear the chest strap all night. And don't laugh—it's been done.)

When you wake up in the morning, moisten the electrode surface on the chest strap and either put it on as you usually do, or hold it in place by clamping your arms down on top of it. Then lie back down and zone out for two or three minutes. If you doze off for a few seconds, that's okay too.

Your heart rate, which will have risen during the rigmarole involved in getting the chest strap in place, will gradually settle back down. Check it from time to time for several minutes, and remember the lowest number you see.

It might be a good idea to write that number down as well, Sparky, in case you doze back off and wake up without a clue about what you've been up to.

And do we even need to stress that any sort of, ahem, strenuous morning activities undertaken before the test will require many minutes of calming down before you can expect anything close to your lowest reading?

Your Morning Resting Heart Rate will vary by a few beats from morning to morning, but if you do this procedure for several days, and you're confident that you're not currently overtraining or coming down with a cold or flu, you'll quickly focus in on the correct number.

As your training progresses, it's a good idea to check your Morning Resting Heart Rate from time to time. If it changes by as much as 5-10 beats and stays there for several days, it would probably be worthwhile to recalculate your Heart Rate Training Chart (see page 33). Otherwise, it's still a good parameter to keep track of and note in your training log from time to time.

Your resting rate will vary with fitness and with temporary conditions

What kind of Morning Resting Rates are normal? It varies quite a bit, but not in the same way that Max Heart Rates do. Many endurance athletes have resting heart rates of 50 or less. Some are under 40, and a very few elite athletes have been measured under 30. One of the truly pleasant aspects of getting in better shape is tracking that resting pulse rate as it gets slower and slower.

6. Calculate Your Training Chart and Set Up Your Monitor "Correctly"

Once you have actual max and resting heart rates, it's a good idea to calculate a complete Heart Rate Training Chart and keep it handy. Assuming you did a good job in getting accurate numbers, this chart will remain an accurate reference for many months or years. You would only want to recalculate if you discovered your Actual Max is a few beats higher, or that your Resting Heart Rate had gone up or down.

The reason a chart is helpful is that, while the most important number you need to know is your 70% Recovery Ceiling, as you get more familiar with the monitor you will want to use it to refine other aspects of your training. Your workout schedule might call for 4 X 800 meters at 90% of max. Or you might want to race a marathon at a nice conservative 75% of max. Most of us would have a hard time keeping the whole array of numbers memorized all the time, and it would certainly be a pain for us mathematically challenged citizens to have to pull out the old number two Ticonderoga every time we needed to calculate a certain percentage of effort.

And in the early stages of heart monitor usage, athletes tend to keep finding out that their actual max or resting rates are slightly different than they had previously thought, so they tend recalculate several times before they get truly comfortable with their own true numbers.

For the computer literate, it's very easy to set up a spreadsheet to compute this chart (see Appendix A, page 216).

Tweaking your numbers in the early going

A Typical Case

Let's go back to our typical 40-year-old runner, Bob Blaster, from the first chapter. We previously guesstimated his Heart Rate Max to be 185, using the general formula of 205 minus one-half his age. We said he figured his Morning Resting Heart Rate was 45. To get his 70% Ceiling, we used the formula (Max HR – Resting HR) X .70 + Resting HR.

That gave Bob a recovery ceiling of 143. To build an entire training chart for this runner, all we'd need to do is use a different multiplier for each level of effort. To calculate 75% of max effort, the formula would be (Max HR – Resting HR) X .75 + Resting HR. To calculate 80% of max effort, the formula would be (Max HR – Resting HR) X .80 + Resting HR, and so on. Here's how Bob's entire chart would look, using his approximated max and resting heart rates.

	PERCENT OF MAX	HEART RATE
	100%	185
Sample	95%	178
chart of	90%	171
a typical	85%	164
runner using	80%	157
estimated	75%	150
numbers	70%	143
	65%	136
	60%	129
	55%	122

Let's say Bob has been running with a monitor for several weeks now, has done the Actual Max Heart Rate Workout, and has faithfully recorded his Actual Morning Resting Heart Rate every morning. In short, he has really zeroed in on his numbers. Let's say he got a 197 on his Max Heart Rate hill workout, and he has consistently seen a Morning Resting Heart Rate of 40. Here is how his chart would look:

	PERCENT OF MAX	HEART RATE
Sample	100%	197
chart of a	95%	189
"high	90%	181
max" run-	85%	173
ner using	80%	166
actual	75%	158
numbers	70%	150
	65%	142
	60%	134
	55%	126

The adjustments necessitated by the Bob's "real numbers" are fairly significant ones. On the low end, he has been really having to reel himself in to stay under 143 (actually, if he has a typical heart monitor which is programmable in increments of five beats, he has probably already allowed himself a couple of extra beats and rounded off to 145). Now he'll be able to run at a much more comfortable 150 and know that he's staying below his 70% ceiling. That's the good news.

On the upper end, Bob's going to find that trying to maintain a heart rate of 173 on a tempo run will be a good bit more challenging than the 164 he previously thought was his Threshold Floor number.

Why actual numbers can be crucial

This case gives you a good idea why it's so crucial to get a handle on your Actual Max Heart Rate and your Morning Resting Heart Rate. A change of five or so beats on your 70% ceiling may not seem like much in an abstract sense, but anyone who trains with a monitor for a while will tell you that a few beats one way or the other can be truly significant in terms of effort and pace, particularly when you're trying to stay below your Recovery Ceiling and when you're edging up toward your maximum effort.

Bob's Actual Max Heart Rate of 197 just happens to fall far enough outside the normal bell curve for the bulk of humanity that the standard formulas don't work very well for him. Does his high max mean that Bob has the potential to be a better runner, or on the contrary, that he may have a dangerous medical condition? Not at all. Your max heart rate is a function both of genetics and of how consistently you've maintained an intense level of exercise over the years. There are many average runners who boast very high Max Heart Rates, and world record holders who have very low ones. The number itself means very little. But identifying the number for each individual runner is extremely important.

Let's take another case to illustrate a case like Bob's, but on the other end of the scale. At running camp one summer, we tested a very good male masters runner, age 40 or so, who happened to have a very low Actual Max Heart Rate. On paper, his numbers should have looked like Bob's approximated chart on page 29, with a 70% Recovery Ceiling of 143 and a Threshold Floor of 164. In fact, his Actual Max was 162! Using a Morning Resting Heart Rate of 45, here's what his chart looked like:

Sample chart of a "low max" runner using actual numbers

PERCENT OF MAX	HEART RATE
100%	162
95%	156
90%	150
85%	144
80%	139
75%	133
70%	127
65%	121
60%	115
55%	109

As you can see, this runner would drive himself crazy trying to use a chart based on standard numbers for his age group. If he were to do a "recovery run" at a heart rate of 143, he would be very close to 85%, which would amount to a very hard tempo run. On his hard day, he would practically kill himself trying to reach his 85% Threshold Floor of 164, because his max is only 162!

144

Of all the runners we've tested over the years, I'd say 80% or more end up with numbers that are pretty close to what the standard formulas predict. The problem is that you can never tell which 20% are going to fall one or more standard deviations

Your Max has nothing to do with ability

outside the "normal" range. It has nothing to do with age, athletic background, natural talent, current fitness level, love life, or creditworthiness. Your own Max Heart Rate is just a number that is personal to you. Once you truly pin that number down—and your Morning Resting Heart Rate—then you can proceed to plan out your training with great confidence that your program is tailored specifically to get the best possible results for you.

So now is the time to prepare your own Heart Rate Training Chart, using your actual numbers. If you want to use a computer spreadsheet to do the calculations (and allow you to change them in the future), see Appendix B on page 216 for information on how to set it up. Otherwise, use the worksheet on page 33.

Heart Rate Training Chart Worksheet

A. ENTER ACTUAL MAX :   _____

B. ENTER MORNING PULSE: _____

C. B minus A to get RANGE: _____

PERCENT OF MAX			RATE
100%	=	A	_____
95%	=	Range times .95 + B	_____
90%	=	Range times .90 + B	_____
85%	=	Range times .85 + B	_____
80%	=	Range times .80 + B	_____
75%	=	Range times .75 + B	_____
70%	=	Range times .70 + B	_____
65%	=	Range times .65 + B	_____
60%	=	Range times .60 + B	_____
55%	=	Range times .55 + B	_____
50%	=	Range times .50 + B	_____

Setting the Monitor Up the "Right" Way

Most monitors allow you to set a zone that beeps when you go above or below it. They usually work in increments of five beats.

Because the most important thing a heart monitor can do is to keep you below 70% on your recovery days, I set up my monitor specifically for that purpose and leave it that way all the time.

Don't set a "zone"; just set your ceiling and be done with it

Rather than picking a "zone" (like 130 to 145) and then having to listen to it beep the whole time I'm running my warm-up or stretching, I set the low end to the lowest number my monitor allows, which is 15. Then I set the high end for my Recovery Ceiling, rounding off to the near five, and just leave it there. I don't worry about running "too slow" on recovery days but I do want to be reminded when I bump up against my Recovery Ceiling. My personal "zone" is thus set at 15 to 145.

On hard days, turn off the infernal alarm!

On days when I'm intentionally running hard, my monitor natually wants to go off early and often, so I just turn the beeper off and glance at the watch occasionally. On days when I'm doing intervals, I always check the monitor as I finish each repeat, to get an objective reading on just how much effort I'm expending. I also check it to see how well I'm recovering during each rest period.

Some people seem to like the details of using a monitor and like to change their settings depending on the workout. My own approach is to treat the monitor as a necessary but bothersome tool and to make its use as trouble-free as possible.

7. Training Yin & Yang: An Overall Approach

Let's take a quick break from our day-to-day training routine to get a bird's eye perspective on where all this heart monitor talk is headed. The essence of this book is built around the "Hard/Easy Principle," which I call "The General All-Purpose Training Principle That Everyone Agrees With But Nobody Follows."

Despite the fact that coaches and runners have been talking about hard/easy for many, many years,[1] there's a good reason that hardly anyone has been able to follow it until recently: It's nearly impossible to do it without a heart monitor.

The foundation of the training system in this book, stated as simply as possible, is this: Many runners (even some very good ones) could vastly improve their training efficiency by running easier (and probably longer) on their easy days and harder (and probably shorter) on their hard days.

The real scoop on hard/easy

Many runners think they're already practicing hard/easy, but they're fooling themselves. The hypothetical case below shows what's really going on.

Our Gal Sal

Here's Sally Strideasy, a 35-year-old good regional age-group runner who's got a PR of 38:00 for 10K. To simplify things, let's say that Sally usually runs around eight miles a day and that she believes she faithfully follows a hard/easy pattern.

She keeps track of her pattern by timing her runs and she knows that she usually averages around 7:30 per mile on her hard days, around 8:00 on her easy days.

A fictional example of the typical runner's program

And yet she complains often that she's too tired to run her planned workout, that she sometimes has to take unplanned days off, and that she seems "stuck" on a performance plateau and hasn't improved her PR in over a year. She feels she's working harder than ever, is more knowledgeable about training than ever, and yet she's not getting any better.

Okay, let's leave aside for a moment Sally's lack of intervals, tempo runs, long runs, and other sophisticated components of a well-rounded training program. Let's concentrate on her overall approach to her training to see where she's going wrong.

Sally is making, in short, the most common error runners make in training. Because she has no objective standard to measure *effort* by, despite her best intentions and efforts, she's running her hard runs too easy and her easy runs too hard until, after a while, all her runs tend to sort of blend together—in terms of effort, if not in elapsed time.

Here's how a typical training session might go. Say she goes out for her hard run on Monday. Maybe she had a short race on Saturday and took Sunday off (or just jogged a couple of miles), so she's fairly well rested and feeling pretty good.

She runs her 8-mile course at nearly a 7:00-flat pace. She knows that's pretty fast for her, but she can handle it. Her schedule called for a hard day, she felt strong, so she put in a good solid effort.

Tuesday is supposed to be an easy day, so she slows down to eight-minute miles, which she thinks of as a complete *jog,* and feels good doing it.

Then she goes out on Wednesday thinking she'll blow out another fast one. To her surprise, even though she feels like she's working harder than she did on Monday, she checks her time and is surprised that she has run 7:40 pace.

"Hmmm," she thinks, "maybe I'm catching the flu."

On Thursday, she goes out for her easy run and has to struggle to run 8:30 pace, which she later finds difficult to believe, since her overall time is very close to the dreaded 70-minute barrier that she considers "unacceptable" for a runner of her ability.

Friday, she's supposed to run hard again but is so exhausted and psyched out, she just hangs it up. She takes a guilty day off from training, holes up with her training diary and a glass of Perrier, trying to figure out where she went wrong.

She finally decides she's just wimpy, lazy, and undisciplined, and she decides what she really needs to do is train harder.

Now, between you and me, Sally is totally, completely, irretrievably *wrong*, but she has absolutely no idea how or when her training went astray.

The big mystery: Where did it all go wrong?

Does Sally's scenario sound familiar? It should. With some variation, it is the same cycle that tens of thousands of runners all over the world go through time and time again. Even some of the most elite competitive runners are not immune, although it may take them several weeks or longer to completely run themselves to a standstill.

☞   *Now, consider this phenomenon: A heart monitor does something even the smartest, most experienced, and most perceptive coach can't do for a runner. It tells the runner the precise moment he starts to go off his program. That's the moment it starts beeping as he bumps up against his 70% Recovery Ceiling that first easy day.*

Let's take a look at what Sally is *really* doing to herself.

On Monday, her hard day, Sally does okay. She's rested and she's due for a hard run. Few runners find it difficult to go hard when they're rested. Her only arguable mistake is going her full eight miles. When doing a "tempo" or Anaerobic Threshold (AT) run, you'll normally want to run anywhere from 20 to 50% shorter than your usual distance.

But we won't be picky. Say Sally did just fine on Monday. She doesn't use a heart monitor (naturally), but if she did, it would show that she was operating at 80-90% of her Max Heart Rate during most of the run. In other words, it was an Aerobic Threshold, or "tempo" run for her.

Her big mistake was Tuesday. She thought that by slowing down to 8:00 pace, she was really giving herself a break. And in fact, it didn't feel too hard of an effort to her. She ran quite a bit slower overall time than she did on Monday (64 minutes instead of 56) so she figured she had done a pretty easy day.

But if she had worn a heart monitor during that run, it would have shown Sally something unexpected: *even running a minute slower than the day before, she was still operating at 80-85% of her max.*

That's right. Because of the effects of her Monday AT run, Sally's body was still dealing with depleted glycogen, leftover lactic acid, and damaged muscle cells. Her Tuesday run, while it may have seemed a good deal slower than her rip-snorter on Monday, was actually *almost the same physiological effort.* And the heart monitor doesn't lie. It doesn't know anything about your "normal" pace or your 10K PR. All it knows is what percentage of maximum your body is currently operating at. And that takes into consideration all kinds of factors you might not be aware of, like: 1. that you're getting a cold, 2. that you're stressed out from work, 3. that you're pregnant, or even: 4. that you shot almost your entire wad on Monday!

When an "easy" day becomes hard

So, to Sally's way of thinking, she's gone hard/easy. A heart monitor would have shown her that she's actually gone hard/semi-hard (see the illustration on page 40).

Now guess what happens on Wednesday? In her mind she should be ready to blow out another hard run. But we now know she's really had two hard days in a row. As we'll see later, the human body can store enough glycogen for about two hours of maximal effort, and it takes a full 48 hours to replace all the glycogen in a fully-depleted body.

Sally's not *out* of glycogen, but she has a lot less of that fuel in her system than she thinks she does (if she thinking about it at all).

When she goes out to hammer on Wednesday, she's going to end up scraping the bottom of the fuel tank, and it's not going to be much fun. On her "easy" Thursday run, she's going to have a hard time, no matter how slow she thinks she's running. She's nearly out of glycogen fuel, but her watch tells her she's running the pace of a beginner jogger, so she puts more effort into it and finishes her "easy" day almost completely exhausted!

No wonder she has to take Friday off. It's supposed to be her hard day, but she can't imagine even jogging, she's so tired. She has no idea what went wrong, and she concludes it's some personal character deficiency.

In reality Sally has been training the whole week in the 80-90% range without knowing it. Instead of hard/easy/hard/easy, she's gone hard/semi-hard/harder/hardest.

The chart below graphically illustrates the problem:

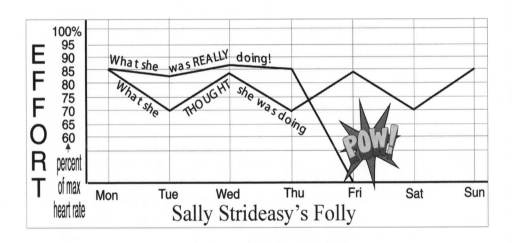

Sally has hit the wall in the same way that marathoners do, except that instead of doing it by running at 90-95% effort for two hours in a race, she's done it by running 80-90% in workouts over four days. She's run out of the muscle's necessary fuel, glycogen, and without glycogen the muscles also cannot burn fat. Everything shuts down until at least some glycogen is replenished.

The Galloway method

It's no wonder that several years ago Jeff Galloway began recommending a minimalist training program that has been much discussed.

Jeff's reasoning is simple: Most runners are going to train too hard on every other day, so simply skip those days altogether. Jeff knows that since it's better to undertrain than to overtrain, why take the chance that the runner will be able to control his pace adequately enough to insure that a recovery day is truly easy, and not an unacknowledged 80-85% day?

A day off is an easy day—too easy

And Galloway is exactly right—as far as he goes. The problem is that you end up "throwing away" half your potential training days, and those are days when you really could be getting in extremely beneficial training. And another problem with this approach is that many runners truly enjoy training, and they don't want to abstain from their sport every other day.

Also keep this is mind: Jeff Galloway did not become an Olympian and world class runner by skipping every other day. He did it by running twice a day, seven days a week, 120-140 miles a week.[2] But guess what? Many of those miles were at a very easy pace.

The early Florida Track Club boasted a number of runners who could easily run right around 5:00 per mile in training runs, but Jack Bacheler, the Olympian who was our mentor, insisted that many of our training miles be run in the 7:00-8:00

*The early
Florida
Track Club
was built on
true
hard/easy
training*

min/mile range.[3] He simply felt that you needed to run that slow in order to truly recover from the hard intervals and AT runs that made up the rest of the program. He also maintained that it was the only way to safely amass the kind of total weekly mileage he felt we should aim for: 100 or more per week. And Bacheler was on two U.S. Olympic teams and was the best U.S. runner at several distances for several years in the late 1960s and early 70s. Bacheler, Galloway and Frank Shorter all ran on the U.S. team in the 1972 Olympics in Munich.

The interesting thing about Bacheler's approach to training was that Florida Track Clubbers could tell other runners about the program in great detail, or writers could describe it fully to their readers, but until runners actually came to Gainesville to run with the group, no one could fully appreciate it. They simply couldn't believe that world class runners would spend so much of their time running so slowly.

*Visitors
couldn't
believe
they ran
that slowly*

And frankly, after all these years of describing this kind of training system to runners, I had finally come to the conclusion that it was just about impossible to get across the point without being there right on the spot, running with athletes and making them SLOW DOWN on alternate days.

It was simply impossible to get across to them just *how much* they really needed to slow down.

*The heart
monitor
doesn't lie*

But now, finally, with the heart monitor, there is an objective standard to go by. The ability level of any given runner is irrelevant. The heart monitor doesn't care and it doesn't lie. We no longer have to get bogged down with "what's your PR?" and "How much have you been training lately?" We can just stay: "Go out and run for 60 minutes at 70% of your maximum." For an elite runner that might be a nine-mile run. For Sally Strideasy, it might be seven. But they'll both be doing the same workout:

putting in essentially the same effort over the same amount of time.

Hard/ easy may also mean hard/ easy/easy

And while we're at it, let's make one minor point. This "hard/easy" approach doesn't have to be a lock-step kind of thing. Some athletes, particularly as they age, may need two or even three recovery days between harder efforts. That's fine. Each runner responds and recovers at a different rate from the stress of hard training. Some may only be able to handle only one hard workout per week. That's okay, too. The crucial point is that all non-hard running should be done at below 70% of maximum heart rate, which will allow for true recovery.

Easy days are also true training days

One final point: We call non-hard workouts "Recovery Days" but they're not meant to just rest your body. In reality we are getting a lot of very important training done on these days. These are not "junk miles." They are not just medicinal. They are an extremely important component of your training.

Permission to go slowly

There are plenty of other benefits from using a heart rate monitor on the "top end" of training, as I'll discuss next, but from my own experience with runners, I've found that it's usually not difficult to get runners to run hard enough on their hard days. The monitor can help you fine tune such workouts, but by far the monitor's greatest benefit is giving runners enough insight into their own physiology to allow them to put the hard/easy training philosophy into practice. And from a psychological viewpoint, it gives them "permission" to go more slowly.

8. The "Yang" Part: Going Hard

Now, let's get back to your training regimen. Let's say you've done your recovery day, and it was so easy you're ready to throttle me. You thought I was probably the biggest coaching quack to come down the pike since Donald Duck and you couldn't believe you'd hang in there for another single day, but you were intrigued by the possibility of proving me wrong, writing a snide letter and getting that gilt-edged apology.

Then you did your Actual Max Heart Rate test and measured your Morning Resting Heart Rate and they weren't too far off from the formulas. And, too, in point of fact you have to admit that I accurately predicted how everything would go, including that ridiculously slow pace you had to run. But now you've calculated your whole Heart Rate Training Chart based on your actual numbers, and you are fairly well convinced that your 70% ceiling really is 145 (or 130, or 155 or whatever), and that there is just the slightest chance that I'm not completely wacko. (If you need a little more reassurance to get you through the next few days, skip ahead and read the case histories in Chapter 11.)

Still hanging in there?

If you're following the program to the letter, you did another recovery run yesterday, the day following your max test, staying below your true 70% Recovery Ceiling and probably muttering the whole time.

So now it's Day Four and finally time for your hard run. If you didn't do any more running after your max test, you've really had three fairly easy days in a row, so you're probably just about ready to bust out of the door and really show your stuff. I can almost picture you, hopping up and down, panting, wanting to know, "What's the workout, coach?"

A little secret about hard days

Now, I'll let you in on a little secret: I really don't much care what you do on your hard days.

It's not that I'm apathetic, it's just that I'm not nearly as worried that you'll blow your training plan on your hard day.

I'll discuss using the monitor during more intense training later in the chapters on setting up training plans, but for now, simply wear the heart monitor and do what you would ordinarily be doing on your hard day. Turn the beeper off, and check your heart rate from time to time to see what kind of numbers you're hitting. If you're doing a tempo run, you should be around 85%. If you're doing intervals, you might be hitting 90-95% toward the middle and end of each repetition.

Generally speaking, your hard days will feel pretty much like most of your runs in your pre-monitor days, except that you should feel a good deal fresher, and you will probably notice your elapsed times for your courses and your interval repetitions will improve.

Turn off the alarm and go!

Okay, for now, head out the door—with that nagging beeper turned off—for your tempo run or your intervals.

Then report back here and we'll discuss what's really going on with this absurdly simple-sounding training strategy.

You know you're a runner when you . . .

. . . are tired, it's late, the weather's lousy and you can't wait to get outside.

9. Reaping the Rewards

O kay, you're back from your tempo run or your interval workout. If things have gone according to plan, you started out feeling pretty well recovered, and you've had a pretty good session.

Now let's talk about how a well-executed heart monitor training program should play out. You already know how I feel about this talk of a "training zone," which is usually defined as 70-85% of maximum heart rate. The problem, as anyone who has used a monitor much can attest, is that there is a *world* of difference between running at 70% of max and running at 85% of max. In fact, it is precisely the difference between a hard day and a recovery day.

The difference between 70% and 85% of max is huge

Yet if you listen to a "training zone" guru, he or she might have you trying to run at 85% every day, which is exactly the mistake Sally Strideasy in Chapter 7 was making as she kept hitting the wall over and over. Actually this so-called "training zone" amounts to a kind of "No Man's Land" of training. You'd be far better off avoiding it altogether by running either above it or below it, which is exactly what our hard/easy approach calls for.

Now, let's move on to the fun stuff.

Say you hang in there with me for a month. What happens?

First, as I mentioned, those torturously slow recovery days start to get faster. Just as you discover that you're enjoying running slower, you find you no longer have to just mope along, you can actually glide along at a fairly respectable clip and still stay below your ceiling. Life is good!

Not only that, you start to find that your hard days are wonderful! You're blitzing your AT runs, you're devouring your intervals, you're laughing out loud as you painlessly finish your long Sunday run (okay, maybe you're not laughing, but you're still pretty happy).

The joys of glycogen surplus

You're discovering the joys of training with plenty of glycogen in your system. As you'll read in the next chapters, your slow recovery days are actually accomplishing a very important goal of distance training: they are teaching your muscles to burn fat rather than glycogen.[1] You're increasing the number and strength of your muscle cells' mitochondria, the little "energy factories" that power your muscles. You're accomplishing a lot more that we can't go into now, but rest assured you're getting a lot more done on recovery days than just "recovering." This all comes under the heading of building that famous "aerobic base" we've heard about for years. Since fat is a much more efficient fuel, the longer and better you can burn fat, the better a long distance runner you will be.

Recovery days are still training days

And you're saving glycogen, which you really *need* for the hard days. As you get up to and over 80% of max, fat won't do it. The hot-burning glycogen takes over more and more of the load. But if you run out of glycogen, you'll hit the wall no matter how much fat you have left. It's one of the hard truths of endurance training: fat won't burn unless there's at least a little glycogen around. (Chapter 10 goes into detail on the science of the body's energy production systems.)

Building an aerobic base, then losing it

A lot of runners build an aerobic base in their early training, then go on to AT runs, intervals, and other anaerobic training. But they make the mistake of running too hard on their "easy" days, which means that they are invading their anaerobic energy supplies to keep up a too-hard pace.

When someone straps a monitor on them and tells them not to go over 70%, they have to crawl to keep their heart rate down. What's happened?

Their aerobic capacity has eroded! They've become more anaerobically fit, but they've lost a lot of their efficient, fat-burning capacity.

All is not lost, of course. They don't have to "start over." But by training with a monitor on easy days at a true recovery pace, they will quickly "backfill" their aerobic capacity once again, and soon be back to running recovery days at a nice comfortable clip. The difference is that it will be taking only 70% of their effort instead of 80% or more.

Backfilling aerobic capacity

At that point, the runner will encounter another interesting phenomenon: *the upper end gets tougher.*

That's right. Sorry to have to report this, but it's not all lilacs and roses. Those 70% days become fun, easy, striding-in-the-country kinds of days, but the 90% AT runs become hell on wheels. Why? Because you're getting in shape. Your body is gaining the capacity to endure previously unimaginable amounts of stress and discomfort.

Your body is becoming a greyhound, but your brain is still a wiener dog.

As your body becomes tougher and tougher, on the hard days you have to push it harder and harder to get the same training effect. Look at it this way:

when you're totally out of shape, it's easy to go out and run 90-95% effort. You're there almost as soon as you leave the door. Just jogging feels "hard," and it is.

It's easy to max out when you're out of shape!

But when you're fit, you've got to really push to get to 90%. It takes a *lot* of concentration to push that hard for long periods of time. In fact, I've known several runners who have been so aerobically fit that they actually had to push fairly hard to run at 75% or 80% of their max heart rates. Imagine being in such good shape that you've got to get psyched up to run what for most is a mere jog. Of course these were exceptional runners with enviable PRs. Most of us usually only have to truly concentrate on paces that are beyond the lactate threshold, which is the point at which our muscle cells are producing more lactic acid that they can either burn up or flush out. That's the point at which the pace starts to hurt, because as everyone knows, lactic acids hurts.

When you're fit it gets harder to reach the peaks

That's why intervals and shorter AT runs are so important for the competitive distance runner to develop his or her potential. By dividing the workout into distinct, manageable segments, the runner develops the concentration to push his training-toughened body into the upper reaches of effort. Just as the mountain climber finds the last 100 feet to the summit orders of magnitude more difficult than the first 100 feet at the base of the mountain, so does the competitive runner find it more and more difficult to push himself to the absolute peak of his condition as his body becomes more and more immune to the doses of exertion he administers.

But that's exactly what is supposed to happen. As your body becomes more efficient at producing energy in the leisurely 70% everyday training ranges, so it also becomes more efficient at propelling you along at the 90 to 95% racing ranges.

The next chapter on the science of training explores in physiological and biological foundation for the training approach described in this book.

10. Why It Works: The Science of Training

(Or: Cooking Out: A Primer on Body Fuels)

Okay, most readers are ready at this point. You have graduated from basic training. Go on, get out of here. Those who are still skeptical about whether any of this is worth their time should turn immediately to Chapter 11 and read some actual case studies to see how other skeptics fared using these methods.

The rest of you have assembled here in the lecture hall because you want to know more about the biophysiology underlying the effective use of the heart monitor. What is so important, after all, about all this glycogen and fat business anyway?

When I give this lecture in person, I always draw two pictures on the blackboard. One is a picture of an outdoor barbecue grill with a big pile of charcoal in it. The other is a can of fire-starter liquid.

Under the charcoal I write "FAT." Under the lighter fluid I write "GLYCOGEN," like so (Pablo Picasso, eat your heart out):

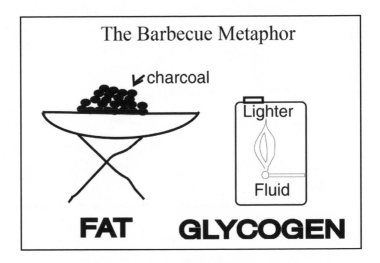

Why train-ing is like cooking out

Here's why the analogy is so apt: You can have a ton of charcoal, but if you're out of starter fluid, the kids are going to be sucking on frozen Oscar Mayers tonight.

You have to have that more volatile starter fuel to get your slower burning charcoal going. Your body is the same way. Glycogen is a hot-burning starter fuel that also *allows* you to burn fat. Your first goal as a distance runner is to learn to rely as much on fat as possible, thus preserving the glyco-gen. When you run out of glycogen, it doesn't make any difference how much fat you have left (and even the skinniest of us have *plenty*, believe me). Again, that situation is known as "hitting the wall." As I pointed out earlier, you don't have to get to the 20th mile of a marathon to hit the wall. Most run-ners sooner or later manage to do it just in the course of training.

Now, with those general concepts in mind, here's the full-blown lecture, reprinted here from *Guide for the Elite Runner* (Seaview Books, 1984), written by Marty Liquori and myself:

It's easy to hit the wall in training

I t has taken many years for the scientists with their test tubes and centrifuges to catch up with what good runners and their coaches have long known from listening attentively to the body's own voices.

In a few instances, the medical world's complete lack of experience with highly trained athletes has led to confusion and unnecessary personal turmoil. One example should suffice to make the point: Australian Kerry O'Brien, a former world-record-holding steeplechaser (a grueling two-mile race over hurdles and a water jump) produced an abnormal electrocardiogram and was told it would be dangerous for him to continue his sport.

Several years later, after many more world-class athletes had been tested on the machine, it was discovered that a large proportion of all elite runners produced graphs which, in a clinical setting, would be cause for alarm.[1]

Why science lags

Scientists and doctors still do not know why highly conditioned hearts dance to such mysterious and unseen orchestras, but they have at long last determined something that anyone who ever raced against Mr. O'Brien could have told them with no sense of irony whatsoever: The gentleman is *not* sick.

As medical researchers and exercise physiologists learn more about the science of exercise, it becomes increasingly clear that upper-echelon runners and coaches have been light-years ahead of the scientists in determining how to develop endurance in the human animal. But while the latest scientific findings have been of little help in fashioning new training techniques, they have provided after-the-fact explanations as to why certain training philosophies and practices (most particularly those of New Zealand's Arthur Lydiard) have been more successful than others.

*A quick
tour of the
research*

With that in mind, we undertake a quick tour of the current scientific knowledge as it relates to competitive distance running.

Although there is some disagreement as to whether this is an oversimplification, most exercise physiologists agree that muscle fiber may be divided into two broad categories, "slow twitch" (ST) and "fast twitch" (FT).

*The fast
twitch,
slow
twitch
business*

The slow muscle cells contract with less force but are more efficient for long-duration work. Each slow cell contains a high proportion of mitochondria, the tiny "energy factories" where fuel is burned with oxygen to create energy and the by-products, carbon dioxide and water, both of which are easily disposed by the bloodstream.

*Lactic
acid and
its effects*

The reason the ST fibers, which have a high oxygen content, are more efficient is that when FT cells create energy without oxygen through an entirely different process, the debilitating by-product lactic acid is formed, and the cells have greater difficulty disposing of it. Lactic acid is the prime cause of fatigue in the shorter distance races (10,000 meters and under).

Just to complicate things a little further, scientists have now found there is an FT muscle cell which is also highly oxidative, like the ST cells. To distinguish them, they call the oxidative FT fiber "fast twitch red" and the non-oxidative FT fiber "fast twitch white." It is helpful to think of the distinction this way: The fast-twitch white cells produce the sudden, explosive energy needed by a sprinter in a 100-yard dash, whereas the fast-twitch red cells can be thought of as a half-miler or miler's type muscles, producing the long, flowing semi-sprint needed to run a mile in four minutes or a half-mile in 1:48. Thus, there are actually three general muscle cell types: slow-twitch red, fast-twitch red, and fast-twitch white.

*Fast
twitch red
cells*

In order to understand the training techniques that follow, it is important to have a working knowledge of each cell type and how it produces energy. Attempts to correlate laboratory findings with practical competitive results are at times confusing, but there can be little doubt that successful distance runners generally have a high percentage of ST muscle, whereas sprinters and jumpers have a predictably high proportion of FT fibers.

In one test in which a muscle biopsy was performed on twenty elite runners in 1972, the average percentage of the body's ST fibers was 79, and several were much higher (up to 98).[2]

The proportion of ST to FT-white and FT-red will likely be shown to be one of the controlling factors in forecasting an individual's potential for success, as well as helping to predict the most promising distance at which to seek the olive wreath.

The magic happens at the cellular level

Once again, good coaches and successful athletes have for many years been unknowingly juggling ST-FT considerations when deciding which event a runner might best be suited for.

"So-and-so is too slow in the quarter to run a really good mile, but he has plenty of strength for the three-mile . . ." is the way the layman-coach might have described an athlete's relative abilities.

Whatever new revelations researchers may have in store for us regarding the various muscle fiber types and their respective roles in energy production, one fact should be very clear to the serious runner: Though the heart, lungs, and digestive system are the most visible and obvious components of the body's energy system, the real secrets behind a 2:09 marathon or a four-minute mile are locked inside the membranes of each individual cell.

There are two distinct kinds of fatigue that will slow or stop the runner. They are so different that runners have evolved separate terms for each, terms that imply (with typical runner understatement) the subtle nuances of each.

The "Bear" versus The "Wall"

"The bear," known to any former track man who has been pressed into unfamiliar duty on his team's mile relay squad, is a debilitating buildup of lactic acid in the muscles. The term can be heard in the following context: "Coming out of the last turn I thought I had him all the way. Then the bear jumped on my back."

Comedian Bill Cosby, in a classic rendition of his own experience on his college mile-relay team, had his own description: ". . . and then . . . all of a sudden . . . *rigor mortis* set in." The condition has also been called "pushing a piano." Whatever one calls it, anyone who has ever been through it knows what it feels like.

The Bear is lactic acid build-up

The "bear" jumps on a distance runner when he has invaded his anaerobic (i.e., non-oxygen-efficient) energy system by running faster than his aerobic (i.e., oxygen-efficient) system can supply energy for. Thus a miler necessarily finishes a race with plenty of glycogen (a sugar, deposited in muscles, which is a main source of energy) left in his system, but with his legs moving painfully through the mire of his own muscle lactates.

For that reason, most middle-distance runners, knowing they will have to invade that anaerobic system heavily during competition, will spend a good portion of their training time on "interval training," which is nothing more than relatively short, fast runs with a prescribed rest period in between. Such training is calculated to toughen the muscles to faster paces, to groove the anaerobic pathways, and to inure the runner to the handling of a lactic-acid load while performing at maximal levels.

The Wall is a lack of glycogen

"The wall" is something altogether different, implying as it does some mystical yet very definitive human barrier from which one staggers away dazed and shaken. Which is precisely the case, of course.

Physiologically speaking, "the wall" is the point at which the runner has depleted his glycogen supplies and must either stop or slow down to the point at which remaining trace energy supplies can handle the demand.

Frank Shorter on the Bear and the Wall

Shortly after winning the gold medal in the Munich Olympic marathon, Frank Shorter made the distinction between the two types of fatigue when he spoke of the last three miles of his victorious race: ". . . I pretty much knew that I had it won at that point, barring a complete breakdown. Right about then, however, your muscles are starting to give out on you. It's not as if the bear's getting you, but you can feel yourself slowly sinking. It becomes a matter of time and physics. It is almost beyond your control . . ."[3]

It is not surprising that Shorter would press the distinction between the two kinds of fatigue on the interviewer. Shorter had himself been primarily a 5000 and 10,000-meter runner until shortly before the games (as well as a competitor in the mile in college), and so would have been all too familiar with the large furry mammal that lies in ambush on the last turn every 400-meter oval in trackdom.

In summary, "the bear" refers to a debilitating oxygen debt brought on by heavy reliance on the anaerobic system, whereas "the wall" is a depletion of the absolutely necessary glycogen fuel (see Figure 1 on page 69).

Ultimately, all distance training is geared toward the production of maximum energy while avoiding both "bears" and "walls."

The three sources of energy

During the course of a long race, the runner's body will rely on three different sources of energy, and it will do so in rather distinct phases. One could think of it almost in the same sense that a car has three forward gears, except for the fact that in the body all three are usually engaged at the same time, but with primary emphasis on only one (see Figure 2 on page 70). Incidentally, in distances longer than the marathon, there are actually more than three stages of energy production.

The "second wind"

For the first few seconds of any strenuous activity, the body gets energy from the anaerobic breakdown of muscle glycogen and blood glucose. That oxygen-less system will operate until the slower-starting aerobic system gets warmed up. This is what is commonly referred to as the "second wind." If the demand for energy is great and the time is short, as in a sprint like the 100-yard dash, the anaerobic system will continue operating until it shuts itself off as a result of lactic-acid buildup.

This shut-off will occur after about two minutes (about the amount of time it takes a good high school half-miler to complete his event) assuming maximum effort.

When the aerobic system kicks in

If the pace is slow enough, the aerobic system begins to shoulder the burden after a few seconds of anaerobic activity. It works by converting muscle and liver glycogen (carbohydrates) into energy by burning them in the presence of oxygen. This produces an efficient high level of energy without the debilitating lactic acid. Instead, water and carbon dioxide are by-products and both are easily carried off by the bloodstream.

One should keep in mind, however, that the anaerobic pathway does not shut down during this phase, but remains available to contribute energy whenever the aerobic pathways cannot handle the demand, such as when the runner encounters a hill, or a surge in the middle of a race. The price one pays for that instant emergency energy, however, is the old bugaboo, lactic acid, which will take several minutes (and several liters of oxygen) to remove. This is often referred to as going into "oxygen debt."

Oxygen debt

Hills and oxygen debt

Every runner knows what oxygen debt feels like. It is the "blown-out" feeling one gets at the top of a hill, a feeling which makes the legs painful and heavy, as if the race should be over already. But after a few moments (sometimes at a greatly reduced pace) the heaviness goes away and one can resume a normal pace again. The runner has simply drawn upon his anaerobic system to handle the hill, incurred an oxygen debt because of it, paid it back as his bloodstream dispersed the lactic acid, and then gone back to the more comfortable aerobic pace. Stage Three comes fully into play after about 30 minutes, of activity when the body begins to utilize fully yet another fuel in the aerobic system: fat. A highly concentrated fuel, fat requires a bit more oxygen to burn than do carbohydrates but the process creates no lactic acid. This fat-burning final stage is *very important* for racing distances between six and twenty-six miles.

Why? Because although fat does not replace glycogen as a fuel during long races, it does serve as an efficient partial substitute, thus forestalling eventual glycogen depletion, which will all but stop the runner.

Out of glycogen equals out of race

Glycogen depletion will bring a runner to an ignominious halt even though he or she still has fat reserves. It seems that burning some glycogen is necessary even when the body is using mostly fat as fuel. One study of a subject on a treadmill for two hours revealed that during the first ten minutes of running, fats contributed 39% of the total fuel, but during the final minutes the figure jumped to 67%.[4]

This fat-burning aerobic phase is the reason so many middle-distance runners engage in marathon-type training during at least part of the year. The more the body can be trained to burn fat, the longer it can forestall the depletion of its glycogen. One study has revealed that a gastrocnemius muscle was seven times more efficient at burning fat after marathon training than before.[5]

"What about breathing?" someone from the audience of a running clinic inevitably asks.

"What about it?" is the equally inevitable response from the guest runner. Or he may be even more flip: "Breathing? I recommend it heartily."

The secret about breathing

Breathing is something that competitive runners do not lose a great deal of sleep about. The reason beginners and novices find it occupying their minds is they feel sure they aren't doing it right. They're having trouble getting enough air into their bodies. They're getting "winded."

What they are really experiencing is the external symptom of an internal cellular problem. It's not that they can't get enough air, but that their cells can't use the oxygen they are getting. The brain interprets this as a lack of oxygen, demands more from the already laboring lungs, and we quickly find the runner panting, "winded."

The answer is not to be found in breathing but in training. There is no substitute for making muscle cells more efficient at burning fuel and oxygen and eliminating wastes. The only good advice that can be given about breathing itself is to relax the face muscles (the blank runner's "mask") and to breathe through the nose and mouth.[6] After that, it's up to your cells.

The heart's role

Although it is generally recognized that long-distance training increases heart size, stroke volume (the amount of blood pumped on each beat), and capillary density, running efficiency finally depends on the muscle cell's ability to use oxygen to burn fuel and eliminate wastes.

How does training affect basic cellular metabolism? Running long distances has been shown to cause an increase in both the number of mitochondria and the secretion of enzymes around the mitochondria which facilitate the fuel-burning process. The mitochondria are where it all happens in aerobic energy production.

Research has shown that increases in mitochondrial and enzyme activity within the cell are directly related to the duration of training runs.[7]

That's *duration*, not intensity. As we will discuss later, this scientifically established fact fits in well with long-established training theories which hold that a "base" of long, relatively slow distance runs should be used to prepare even the half-miler for competitive running.[8] Indeed, there is nothing more basic to distance running than beefing up the cell's ability to use oxygen in the mitochondria.

Duration of training is key to fat burning

Research has demonstrated that ten minutes of running is necessary to increase an oxidative enzyme by 10% in rat muscle (which is similar to that of humans'), whereas 30 minutes would cause a 30% increase, 60 minutes a 40% increase, and 120 minutes a 100% increase in the same enzyme. But training in excess of 120 minutes was actually counterproductive, leading to exhaustion and the inability to attain even formerly achievable goals.[9] This finding is in accordance with current training theories which hold that maximum benefits from training are derived by running between 80 and 140 miles per week, and that training in excess of these distances will not likely be beneficial, and could be counterproductive.

Running longer than two hours is counterproductive

Increasing the number and efficiency of the mitochondria is especially important for the longer races because the greater the number of mitochondria, the less each one has to be stimulated to begin burning fat instead of glycogen. In short, the muscle cell arrives at the most efficient third stage of energy production earlier in the run and thus conserves the all-important glycogen for later effort. And in the longer distances (as opposed to the middle distances, where lactic acid buildup is the limiting factor) it is the depletion of glycogen which slows or stops the competitor.

*The differ-
ence
between
middle
and long
distance
races*

*The heart
adapts
dramati-
cally*

*The heart
is a totally
cardiovas-
cular
muscle*

Whether they put it in scientific terms or not, nearly every knowledgeable coach and runner these days uses long, relatively easy training runs as an early-season base for the overall aerobic conditioning of middle and long-distance runners. They are merely building up the mitochondrial activity in each cell, preparing for future demands, putting off as long as possible the eventual collision between the runner and the "wall."

Although the body's most important and fundamental adaptations to training occur at the cellular level, the most obvious changes to the observer (whether casual or scientific) involve the enhancement of the oxygen transport system, i.e., the lungs, heart, blood, arteries, capillaries, and veins.

Perhaps the most dramatic transformation of all is that of the heart, whose pulsating walls grow thicker and stronger, and whose overall size increases measurably with training. The late Steve Prefontaine's heart, for instance, was 30 to 40% larger than that of a normal adult his size.[10] And it has been reported that the great Paavo Nurmi, the "Flying Finn" of the 1920s, was powered by a heart nearly three times normal size.[11] Once again, experimentation with animals gives confirmation; it has been shown that rats experience measurable cardiac enlargement with as little as 10 minutes daily training.[12]

Although an enlarged heart would be cause for alarm in a clinical setting, it is quite normal among runners. The heart is, after all, perhaps more innately suited to distance running than any other group of muscle fibers in the body. It is composed entirely of slow-twitch, highly oxidative muscle fiber, and even in an untrained state has an extremely high mitochondrial content and a dense system of blood vessels. One way of looking at it is to consider that the heart is the one muscle that is always doing aerobic work, even when the body is at rest. Since it has probably already achieved, in an untrained state, its most efficient cellular adaptation through simple evolution (in other words, the heart cannot increase its mitochondrial activity through training), the only avenue left for adaptation to the increased demands of distance running is simply to grow larger and stronger.

The trained heart beats much slower

The trained heart does this so well that it beats less often—both at rest as well as during exercise—than the same untrained heart, while actually increasing the amount of blood pumped per beat. When the heart is doing submaximal work, the overall flow of blood is actually decreased by training because the now more efficient muscle cells simply extract more oxygen from the bloodstream than they could before training.

Changes brought about by training are less dramatic (but equally important) in the other components of the oxygen delivery system. For all the novice's worry over "wind" and breathing techniques, the lungs appear to undergo only minor adaptations, the primary one being an enhanced ability to exchange carbon dioxide for oxygen in the air sacs (called a lower "alveolar-arterial oxygen gradient"). The vital capacity (amount of expellable air that lungs can hold) can be measurably enlarged when training is initiated during childhood, or when it takes place over a long period of time,[13] although some authorities hold that experiments (probably short term) with adults show no such increases.[14]

As mentioned previously, elite runners do not waste any time worrying about breathing rhythms or techniques. Difficulties in that area are generally reflective of more basic adaptive problems, usually a lack of anaerobic work in training and a consequent distressing oxygen debt in the early part of a race.

Training increases blood supply

It takes time to grow capillaries

Training increases an individual's overall blood supply markedly, and thus increases the total supply of oxygen-carrying hemoglobin, which is found in the red blood cells. That's why there was so much hoopla in the late 1980s about allegations that some athletes were exploiting this phenomena by reinfusing their own stored blood, or "blood doping."

But probably the most important—as far as ultimate racing success—adaptations in the oxygen delivery system occur in the extreme far reaches of its labyrinth-like network, in the millions of tiny capillaries which carry the oxygen-laden red cells to the muscles, one at a time. Simply put, distance training seems to promulgate a more diverse and efficient profusion of those tiny tubes, and scientists have found that this leads to a significant increase in blood distribution to muscles when they are engaged in maximal effort.[15]

Because a superior capillary system probably requires more time to develop than any of the other cellular or cardiovascular adaptations, it is probably the reason that the process of developing a world-class distance runner takes a minimum of three to four years. (And it has been often cited as one of the chief reasons that the Kenyans—who begin distance running as toddlers—become such gifted competitors.)[16]

The fondest dreams of Hollywood screenwriters notwithstanding, a sedentary accountant doesn't quit his job, run a few miles on the beach with a dog, and then make the Olympic team. People who are going to succeed in distance running are like the coal-burning locomotives from days of yore: You can see them coming from a long way off.

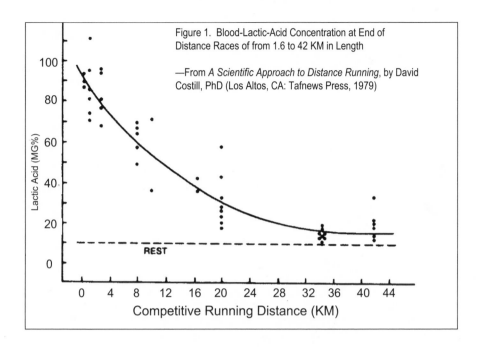

Figure 1. Blood-Lactic-Acid Concentration at End of Distance Races of from 1.6 to 42 KM in Length

—From *A Scientific Approach to Distance Running*, by David Costill, PhD (Los Altos, CA: Tafnews Press, 1979)

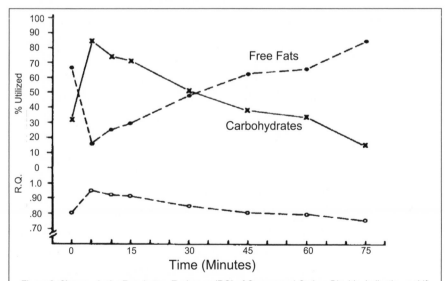

Figure 2. Changes in the Respiratory Exchange (RQ) of Oxygen and Carbon Dioxide, indicating a shift of the utilization of carbohydrates and fats by the working muscles —From *A Scientific Approach to Distance Running*, by David Costill, PhD (Los Altos, CA: Tafnews Press, 1979)

11. Case Studies: Hey, It Really Works!

S o counterintuitive do many runners find the training system described in this book that the biggest hurdle I often face is convincing them that it will actually work. In that regard, no argument has proven quite so persuasive as personal success stories from fellow runners. Therefore, I am including the following actual training and racing accounts, told in the athletes' own words.

How I Ran 20 PRs in 25 Races

Jack Gescheidt

by Mark Guralnick

(The author is a market research analyst for Gannett's USA Weekend in New York. Just for fun, on weekends he works at the Super Runner store on Amsterdam Avenue. He lives in Brooklyn with his wife, Joanne. This article appeared in the January 1996 issue of Running Times. *Reprinted by permission of the author.)*

In June 1993, an appealing challenge was presented to me at the Maine Running Camp: If I invested in a heart rate monitor and obeyed its electronic message, it was guaranteed that I would improve my racing times. And, as contradictory as it may seem, this would be accomplished by training at least part of the time at a *slower* pace. I was 36 years old at the time and had been running for five years, averaging 20-25 miles per week. I was ready to try a new approach that would improve my running, but I didn't want to commit myself to a program that would feel like a second job.

I had begun running in the spring of 1988 after several years of a fairly sedentary life. My employer was recruiting us to participate in a 3.5-mile race in Central Park called the Corporate Challenge. I talked two road running friends into "whipping me into shape." Within two weeks I was running the 3.5 mile distance. After completing the race that June, I was hooked. The racing atmosphere and the joy of competing filled a void in my life.

I kept running, but after several years, I became a little frustrated. My performances were okay, but they had definitely plateaued. I found myself wondering how much better a runner I could become if I really applied myself. Heart monitor training appeared to be a very rational, safe and methodical way to find out. That's what made it so appealing to me.

Getting Started

Because little else has changed in my training, I believe that most of my successes over the past two years can be attributed directly to the heart rate monitor. Just strapping it on, however, did not make me run faster. It was more complicated than that.

The first step was to determine accurate ranges for different types of workouts: speed, tempo, long and recovery runs. My maximum heart rate was determined during a track workout (using a borrowed heart rate monitor) conducted at the Maine Running Camp. The specific ranges (zones) were calculated on a computer using formulas recommended by coach John Parker, a well known heart rate monitor proponent.

Step two was to devise a weekly training schedule. I had no specific race goal, just to run faster in the 5K-10K distances I usually raced, along with an occasional 10-miler. We set up a program of five sessions per week: one speed/hill workout, one tempo run, one long run and two recovery runs. Although I was running only about 20-25 miles per week, it was almost all quality, and I knew the purpose of every single workout.

The Initial Shock

I was told that the key would be patience and discipline. Patience, because I would see no benefits for at least a month. Discipline, because on recovery days I would have to ignore my slow pace and let every other runner (yes, *every* runner) go by. Both of these predictions came true. But I figured if

I was not willing to give the monitor the amount of time and effort needed to work its alleged magic, then I shouldn't have purchased it in the first place.

Many runners have days where they do "recovery" or "easy" runs. My experience soon convinced me that without a monitor, most runners are training too hard to get the intended benefits. For example, my "easy" run back then was usually one 3.4 mile loop of Prospect Park near my Brooklyn home. Before using a monitor, this "easy" run would take me 25-26 minutes (about 7:25 per mile). The first four times I ran it using the monitor at under 70% of my max (144—which coach Parker calls my "Recovery Ceiling"), it took me 30-32 minutes! As if that wasn't frustrating enough, I had to stop and walk each time I came to the one hill on the loop because I was unable to keep my heart rate from shooting up over 144.

I couldn't even cheat effectively. I raised my "Recovery Ceiling" to 152 (75% of my maximum) thinking I wouldn't have to stop to walk, but this strategy didn't work either. Could it be that I was really not very fit? I followed a good diet, ran 20-25 miles a week, and generally felt I was in good aerobic shape. But the heart rate monitor was telling me a different story.

The embarrassment peaked one day on my "long" run (at that time was 6.7 miles). My usual 53-minute run took 69 minutes! I stopped to walk six times. My wife, Joanne, joined me for this run, but not for long. In the past we had avoided training together because her pace was too slow for me. Not any more. The monitor told me in no uncertain terms that Joanne was running too fast for me.

Even though I had to admit that I was getting a little depressed, there was no place for me to go but up. I certainly couldn't get any slower: I was already walking!

Breakthrough

Week after week, the pattern repeated itself. I was running very slowly with no apparent improvement indicated by my heart rate. I even had to wake up earlier in the morning to run so I wouldn't be late for work. Finally, in early September 1993, after six weeks of heart rate monitor use, it happened. I completed a Prospect Park loop in 28:50 on a recovery day and the heart rate hadn't surpassed 75%. I had my breakthrough. Within a few weeks I was able to drop my recovery ceiling back to 70% and still run at what felt like a reasonably brisk pace.

All this time, however, the flip side of the recovery runs was the harder stuff: speed workouts and tempo runs. Running hard caused my heart rate to soar instantly. But that began changing, too. As my fitness improved, getting my heart rate up to the 90-95% interval zone and 80-85% tempo zone became more and more difficult. It became hard work again.

Every Tuesday night after work, I participated in organized speed and hill workouts in Central Park conducted by a group called Personal Best. These workouts built my leg speed and strength. The heart rate monitor's role was to push me into the 90-95% zone to get the maximum benefit. Without the monitor, there had been nights when I was disappointed if my times in half-mile repeats weren't consistent. Now I concentrated on lifting my heart rate into the 90-95% zone and not worrying as much about time. The key was effort, which the heart rate monitor displayed unerringly on my wrist. The training seemed to be working as planned, but the real test would be racing. I couldn't wait.

The 1993-1994 Racing Season

Six months after strapping the heart rate monitor on for the first time, this new and improved runner was ready for his first race: the January 1994 Northwind 10K in Central Park. It was an unimpressive debut for the "new Guralnick." My 44:12 finish was only 18 seconds off my PR, but after all this meticulous heart rate monitor training, I wanted instant results. On the other hand, the footing was terrible due to icy conditions, so the weather provided the inevitable handy excuse.

But I didn't sulk long. The following weekend was the annual Super Bowl 5K, also in Central Park. There is no easy course in Central Park, whether a 5K or half marathon. There are hills that range from "gently rolling" to "oxygen debt specials." This 5K course is run on the upper loop of the park and includes the toughest hills. Despite the terrain, however, I ran my first PR since beginning heart monitor training: 20:41, a 31-second improvement over my previous best, which was run on a considerably easier course.

Ironically, I did not wear the heart rate monitor during the race. Racing with a monitor, I felt, gave me one more thing to be concerned about during the race. I felt more comfortable reading my performance by the mile splits and listening to my body. (A race is about the only time you'll find me running without a monitor, however; most of the time, it's glued to me.)

My next shot at a 10K came in late March on the same course as the January 10K in Central Park. It was difficult to maintain my training in the January-March period because of the snowy, icy conditions of one of the worst New York winters in memory. However, I was still hopeful of running well at the Rites of Spring 10K. Once again, the training plan paid off. This time I set a 36-second

PR (43:18).

This performance began a trend that continues to this day: setting personal records an average of four out of every five races that I run. The actual numbers are 20 PRs out of my last 25 races. These race achievements parallel the progress of my training runs. Times for my recovery runs, long runs and tempo runs all dropped. They were still generally not as fast as I had run before using the monitor, but this was because I wasn't wasting valuable energy pushing myself on so-called "easy" days. My truly hard efforts were saved for races.

Running slower on the easy days did not mean simply ignoring my training times. Since every improved training time meant an improvement in conditioning, I still got excited about setting PRs on easy runs while staying under my recovery ceiling. However, recovery run PRs did not happen frequently. Some plateaus lasted six months or more before a new training breakthrough.

After the Rites of Spring 10K, I went to Washington, D.C. for the Cherry Blossom 10-miler in early April. This was only the second time I ever raced this distance, and the result was a two minute PR (1:11:11). Five weeks later, I broke my 5-mile PR by 1:38 at the Alamo Alumni Run in New York (33:09). The following week I reduced my 5K PR by 31 seconds to 20:10 in another Central Park race. This completed the most satisfying stretch of racing I had ever experienced. From late January through late May 1994, I set PRs at four different distances: 5K, 5 miles, 10K and 10 miles.

Ecstatic, I returned to Maine Running Camp in late June with logbook statistics in tow. The coaches offered their congratulations and suggested that we not change my program for the next year. They promised that my results would continue to improve if I stayed the course. They were correct.

1994-1995 Racing Season

Throughout the summer months I did no racing. The heat and humidity of the New York City area this time of year zaps my strength and motivation to race. But the heart rate monitor training continued. In August I increased my long run in anticipation of the Philadelphia Distance Run (half-marathon) on September 18th. The monitor readings in the last few miles of these training runs rose to the mid-to-upper 150s (close to 80% of my maximum). This was a warning to ease up: my body was not ready to run 13 miles at my 10-mile training pace. After a couple of more 13-mile runs, my heart rate actually began to *decline* in those last few miles.

The Philadelphia race brought me a 29-second PR (1:36:27) over my only previous half-marathon. The Philadelphia race inaugurated a year of race results that would surpass even my 1993-1994 performance.

In early October, a new training breakthrough occurred. My usual time for a five-mile recovery run (in the 65-70% zone) dropped by a minute to the 42-43 minute range. I had come a long ways since the days I had to stop and walk to keep my heart rate down. At the beginning of my heart rate training in July 1993, this same five-mile run in the 65-70% zone had taken me two to three minutes longer.

The faster training within the recovery zone had a positive impact on my race results. On Thanksgiving Weekend I ran a 32:47 for 5 miles, a two-minute improvement from my 5-mile best before heart monitor training.

A few weeks later, I lowered my 10K best by 1:42 to 41:36, and in January 1995, I broke 20 minutes in a 5K for the first time (19:52). By March, my 10K time would stand at 41:17 and by Memorial Day, two more 5K PRs brought my best to 19:25.

The highlights of the winter/spring 1995 racing season were two 10-mile runs: the Pear Blossom in Medford, Oregon, and the Broad Street Run in Philadelphia. The Pear Blossom was held April 8th in raw, 36 degree weather. It rained all night and did not stop until five minutes before race time. A little past halfway, the rain started again, but it was too late to spoil my race. I ran a 1:07:42, a 3:39 PR over the Cherry Blossom performance a year earlier. This PR lasted only four weeks. At the Broad Street Run, I lowered that PR by another 1:43 to 1:05:59. My 10-mile time dropped by 5:13 in a little over a year.

No Smoke, No Mirrors

These results came from no innovative workouts, changes in diet, or special potions. It came from trusting the target zones of the heart rate monitor and doing one speed/hill workout, one tempo run, one long run (usually 10 miles) and two five-mile recovery runs every week, all in the appropriate zones.

Recovery runs of 5 miles take me 42-43 minutes (8:35 per mile pace) to complete at 65-70%, a tempo run at 80-85% is run at about 7:35 pace, and racing 5 miles is done at 6:33 pace. This is the most important lesson to me. Training with the heart rate monitor allows me to recover well from hard workouts on "easy" days, control the effort on hard or long days, and to save my energy for excelling in races, where it really counts.

It certainly wasn't an *easy* program to implement in the early going, in the sense that it took a lot of discipline to run either slow enough or fast enough to stay in the appropriate zones. But I was mentally well prepared for these phenomena, and I stuck it out.

And since 80% of my races result in PRs, do you need to ask if it was all worth it?

Summary

In my two years of training with a heart rate monitor, I believe I realized three primary benefits:

• **Impressive Race Results:** My 5K time has dropped from 21:12 to 19:07; 10K—43:54 to 41:17 and 10 miles—1:13:11 to 1:05:59.

• **Running Easy During Most Training Runs:** I know, it defies logic that you can become a faster runner by running slower. But it happened to me. Three of my five weekly runs are done at a pace that looks as if I am out for a recreational run instead of a serious workout. It also feels good to run easy. Instead of gasping for air at the end of each morning's training run, I am refreshed and ready to start my work day. My reward for taking it easy on recovery days is a slew of PRs.

• **Running Injury Free:** Because the heart rate monitor generally makes my training paces slower, I have been running injury free. Easy running has been easy on my legs. I run hard twice a week (one speed/hill workout, one tempo run) and I race 12-15 times per year. This balance has kept me injury-free on the roads for two straight years. I know many runners who frequently break down because they run too hard too often. These runners often pass me on training runs, but rarely do so in races.

Update:

Since the original publication of this article in *Running Times* in January of 1996, my heart monitor-based training has continued to bring steady racing success and new PRs. Below is a summary of new PRs.

1996

3/24	Brooklyn Half Marathon	1:33:20
4/13	Run for Aspire 10K	41:14

1997

3/8	Brooklyn Half Marathon	1:32:22
11/23	Philadelphia Marathon	3:31:30

1998

4/26	Rockaway Ocean Run (5 mi.)	31:33
5/7	Corporate Challenge (3.5 mi.)	22:58

1999

10/9	Corporate Challenge (3.5 mi.)	22:54

October, 1999

A Serious Skeptic

by Paula Huntsman

(The author is a 37-year-old nurse in upstate New York, a former high school state champion, and a mother of two.)

I was a camper at the Maine Running Camp in the summer of 1997 when I saw my first heart rate monitor. I had no idea what it was or why anyone would need one, and frankly I didn't care. I figured it was a gadget that I could do without. My running had been coming along nicely, so I figured, why complicate things? Little wonder I've been called a knucklehead on more than one occasion.

My running career started when I was cut from the basketball team as a junior in high school. I joined the indoor track team and ran my first race, a 600-yard dash, with no training at all. I placed third and was hooked. I eventually enjoyed a successful high school running career, culminating with a first in the state two-mile my senior year. But that was 1979 and a lot has happened since then.

I continued to run sporadically for the next sixteen years, but mostly for my own enjoyment; I raced very little, but when I did, it seemed that despite my advancing years, I still had some potential in this crazy sport. For instance, just after my second son turned six months old, I trained for a month and ran a local 10K, finishing fairly well in 50 minutes.

But along about then I discovered something else about running. I discovered that training fulfilled a desperate need I had for time that I could call my own, a precious daily respite from the frantic, wall-to-wall responsibilities of raising two energetic little boys.

So, in the summer of 1993, I began to run seriously again. I joined the throngs of people training for a marathon. I cut out a "Train for a Marathon in 13 Weeks" schedule from a running magazine and followed it exactly.

The results weren't pretty. In my first marathon I went out too fast and didn't drink enough before or during the race. By mile 18, I was so dizzy the runners in front of me appeared blurry. I finished in 3:38, walked over to where my family was waiting in a big, trampled-down field, and just laid down in the mud.

When I regained consciousness in the medic tent I realized I had qualified for the Boston Marathon. I'd love to tell you I learned from my experience and did things completely differently the next time, but, well, I'm a knucklehead. I trained as before, went out too fast and by mile 18, I was fading fast. I finished in 3:35, just a bit faster than my first marathon, but feeling about as bad. Fortunately, the finish area around the Boston Marathon is all paved, so at least I didn't end up sleeping in the mud.

But I was disappointed I hadn't run a smarter race. Then later that spring, I ran a 19:48 5K and lowered my 10K time to 40:22, a PR by 2 minutes. So I was still convinced I had some good races in me, and decided that what I needed was some professional guidance. I signed up for the Maine Running Camp later that summer.

That was when I was first exposed to the heart rate monitor, and as I say, I wasn't exactly an instant convert. I ran mostly at my own pace during the runs and I went to all the training talks.

I heard 70%, 70%, 70%, but I didn't really comprehend exactly what they meant. I thought I probably already trained at around 70%; at least it certainly seemed like about that kind of effort. I watched the other campers play with the heart rate monitor and I teased them. I remember thinking, I'm a *nurse,* why do I need an expensive gadget to take my *pulse?*

I finally did succumb to curiosity and consented to play with a loaner monitor one day. I was surprised to feel how slow running at 70% of my max really was. And the other news flash was that after a long run my own professional pulse-taking ability was somewhat inaccurate! I also found that my resting HR was a little slower and my max HR was a lot higher than I had expected.

Convinced that there might be more to this training business than I had originally figured, I decided to hire a private coach. When I went in to see him for my first consultation, he simply handed me a piece of paper that said: "6-10-6-10-6-Off-10, all at 70%."

That seemed like a pretty tall order. From my brief experience with the monitor I already knew how hard it was to stay under 70%. And from my own training, I knew that I hadn't run anywhere near that kind of mileage. But if I was going to pay someone to coach me, I was certainly going to do as he asked. On the last day of camp I finally bought my own heart rate monitor. Without taking it out of the box, I shoved it in my suitcase and headed home.

Back at home, still excited from what I had learned at camp, I went off to do my first long run with a monitor. It started beeping by the end of my driveway! I was over 70% before I actually got on the road! Then it beeped on *every* hill I encountered and sometimes it beeped on completely flat, level road!

My loop took me almost twenty minutes longer than it used to before the heart rate monitor. I had to run *pitifully* slowly to keep the darn thing from beeping! I called my coach and told him that the term "70% effort" should refer to leaving 70% of your ego at home!

The next day I met up with my running partners and showed them my new toy. They were skeptical, of course. It was just another gadget that they didn't need.

They ran the first mile with me then left me in the dust. We had logged a lot of miles together and respected one another quite a bit, so I was astonished when the group didn't simply listen to me and follow my advice!

Instead they said, "We liked the old Polly better, the one that would run fast with us."

As the weeks went on, they continued to heckle me, circling around, rolling their eyes, and then running off into the sunrise. And because I am a knucklehead, there were days when I'd turn off the alarm and run after them. But, for the most part I trusted my coach and let them go on without me. For a month I just did 70% runs of varying distances during the week, and a long run on the week-end. The actual running felt fine. I wasn't too tired and I didn't have many aches and pains. I did get "sleepy" tired because I do all of my running early in the morning before the boys are awake.

Soon I started noticing changes. My 70% runs weren't taking as long as they had been. My mileage was up from 35 miles a week to a solid 50. And, I felt *good!* I felt strong and I was actually enjoying my runs more often. And I was enthusiastic about my running. I was really looking forward to testing my new strength.

Finally my coach had me start some track work. I purposely didn't bring a watch, so I don't know how fast I was going, but just to get back to some fast running felt grand!

When the fall racing season came around I was curious to see what would happen.

My first race was a 5-miler, and I didn't wear my heart rate monitor (after all it's for *training,* right?). I went out for the first mile in 5:45 (you may notice a trend here) and hung on, painfully, to the bitter end, averaging about 6:30.

I blew it and I knew it. For my next race, a 10K, I decided to wear my heart rate monitor. This time I went out in 6:10, ran evenly through the race, and finished in 41:30, a full 1:30 faster than I had run the previous year at the same race. Now *that* was more like it! It was a mountainous course but I kept my perceived effort throughout the race at a tolerable level. None of the "Oh-I'm-going-to-drop-puke-or-die" feelings.

The next race for me was a 15K. Again I wore my heart rate monitor, went out at a controlled pace and actually *enjoyed* myself in a race! I went through 5K in 19:20, 10K in 40:30 and finished in 61:40. A recent PR at 5K, a near all-time PR at 10K and a 2-minute improvement at 15K, all in the same race. The program was working!

Winter's are early and harsh in upstate New York where I live and my racing season ended in October. I did easy mileage through the Christmas season. Slowly, my mileage has built up to the 60-mile weeks I'm doing now, as I write this.

I'm currently doing a weekend long run, two long-ish runs during the week, one tempo run and two to three easy days. My whole mind set has changed. I used to consider 10-12 miles "long," now long is 15-18 miles. I run controlled enough to enjoy the mileage and my long runs no longer render me into a blithering idiot. I truly run at 70% of my maximum, except for hills, where I allow myself to cheat up to 75-80%. The first few tempo runs after a winter of slow comfortable running were pretty miserable.

My lungs and legs burned, but now the air is

warmer and I'm used to tempo runs again. It's not all rosy, I've made some compromises in my lifestyle to accommodate more time spent running. I haven't done my usual skiing this winter. I tend to sleep more hours a night and my legs ache walking up the stairs.

My running partners haven't become the converts I hoped. One of the women knows I'm on to something. She hasn't said it out loud but she trains with me without question. When I go slow, she's beside me. When I run long, she runs long. Speed work? She's game. One of the guys continues to be skeptical, saying things like, "Oh, are you still training with that monitor?" The others quietly do their training and let me do mine. They win most every training run, but not the races! As spring approaches, I'm looking forward to racing again. In my first race of the season, with no intense training at all, I managed a 40:44 10K and was first woman, an encouraging start! My plan is to run shorter races until I turn 40, then maybe try another marathon (and this time do it right).

But of course, like most runners, my real goal is simply to see how good I can get. And now, instead of just winging it—as I was doing a year ago at this time—I'm confident that I've discovered a system that will allow me to realize that goal.

I may be a knucklehead, but I'm no dummy!

Update:

Okay, so now I call myself a Recovering Knucklehead: I take it one day at a time. I've had success when I use the monitor correctly. I've had disasters when I've cheated.

After the above was written, I was training 50-60 miles a week and feeling quite strong, I started running with the local high school girls. The problem was that I was doing *my* workouts in the morning and *theirs* in the afternoon. I also fell off the knucklehead wagon in another way: I started running hard again with my regular running buddies, and frequently.

Nonetheless, I ran my first race in the spring of '98 at close to my PR of 40:30. The next race, I went out too fast and crashed. I saw very little improvement over the spring. I was discouraged and angry and was naturally blaming my coach when I showed up for that summer's running camp.

He pointed out that I had no one to blame but myself. After getting reindoctinated into the heart monitor mentality I headed home to "do it the right way" this time. I went back on strict 70% recovery days. That fall, I broke 40 for 10K for the first time and PR'd at 15K! *Finally*, it was really working. The racing took its toll though, so I did base miles all winter, and when spring came around I still didn't have the hunger to race. I just stayed on the plan and did my miles, but at least I had some company. My running partners had finally come around and were willing to run with me!

Then in mid-summer I ran a large international 15K. I had a PR by a minute and placed second in my age group! But I still didn't have much of a desire to race, so I decided to just keep training and aim for a fall marathon. Gradually increasing both mileage and intensity, as well as adding a weekly long run that slowly grew from 16 to 22 miles, I stayed strictly on the monitor for recovery days.

Then in October of 1999, I ran the wonderful Twin Cities Marathon, staying right on 80% for the first 20 miles, as instructed. As my coach had told me, it felt so incredibly easy it was hard to convince myself it was the right pace.

It was. I ran a 3:14:02, a 21-minute PR!

October, 1999

Heart of the Runner

artwork: Rossie Newson

by Jeff Testerman

(The author is a staff writer for the St. Petersburg Times. *This article appeared in the June 5, 1994 edition.* ©*1994,* St. Petersburg Times, *used by permission.*)

Late last year, I felt stuck in the running doldrums. I was training harder than ever without getting faster at any distance. My PRs in road racing were distant memories. I turned to technology. At Christmas, I shelled out $100 for a heart-rate monitor. Then I picked up a tiny tract by running writer John L. Parker, Jr. with the endearing title *Heart Monitor Training for the Compleat Idiot.*

Parker, a former world-class runner at the University of Florida, offered this guarantee: "Give me a month, two if possible, and if you're not running, racing and feeling better than you ever thought possible, send this book back to me, and I'll send you a refund and a certificate of apology suitable for framing."

I never got that refund.

I tried Parker's heart-rate monitor training program for two months, then stepped up to the starting line in late February to test his theory. A few weeks later, I had obliterated my PRs at the 5K, 10K and 15K distances.

Not just by a little. I lowered my 10K PR by 47 seconds. I shattered my 15K best, a record set almost three years earlier, by 75 seconds.

For someone who passed into the Masters (age 40) and Clydesdale (more than 200 pounds) categories years ago, this was euphoria, new life, the realization that, okay, maybe I was getting older and thicker around the middle, but I was also getting faster and, in a cardiovascular sense, fitter. And I was doing it with fewer training miles fewer aches and pains and no injuries.

Parker's hypothesis, though oriented toward distance running, is applicable to cycling, swimming or any activity aimed at aerobic fitness. Athletes get best results, he says, if they alternate hard days with recovery days. And the best way to do that is with a heart rate monitor.

"The average runner runs too fast on slow days and then can't run fast enough to really improve on his fast days because he's burnt out," says Dr. David Martin, a human performance specialist who works with world-class runners at Georgia State University. "The heart rate monitor is an indicator of how you're handling the stress load—the combination of your fitness level and environmental factors like heat, humidity or hills."

A caveat for those considering heart rate monitor training: Experts caution that no one should take up an exercise program, particularly a strenuous one, without first seeing a physician.

The heart rate monitor I picked out is the Favor, a basic model made by Polar, a Finnish company that boasts an 80% market share of wireless monitors sold in the United States. Polar uses electrocardiogram-accurate electrodes encased in a chest band that pick up the heart's electrical impulses, then transmit them to a receiver on a wrist band.

The chest band is water-resistant, lightweight, adjustable and easy to wear for men or women. The receiver, which looks like a watch, displays heart rate, expressed in beats per minute, and a tiny heart that pulsates at the same rate as your heart. The receiver is turned on when placed next to a chest band in place. It turns itself off automatically when the chest band is removed. Polar says its transmitter battery won't need replacing for 2,500 hours.

The unit can feed back false readings if the monitor is in range of electromagnetic signals. On my first day wearing the monitor, I got, uh, quite a jolt when I ran under some high-tension lines and saw a heart-rate readout of 240.

So how do you interpret heart rate, then control it for optimum training?

First, calculate your maximum heart rate. You can do get a temporary estimate using an age-based formula, but Parker recommends that you eventually do a "Max Heart Rate Workout" to get a more accurate number.

Now, you're ready to calculate what Parker calls your "recovery ceiling" and "threshold floor."

First, figure 70% of your max. That's your recovery ceiling, the maximum heart rate your should maintain on easy training days. Parker suggested that 70% may seem slow for most runners, and he was right. Initially, I had to slow down, really rein it in, to stay at my recovery ceiling.

Next, calculate 85% of your maximum heart rate. That's your threshold floor, the minimum heart rate you should maintain during your run on hard training days. Eighty-five percent output is a tough run, I found, about like running an all-out 10K race. I'm a morning runner, and I kept these hard runs down to about half the distance of my easy runs so I wasn't exhausted coming in to work every other day.

The schedule that worked for me was a three-mile run at pell-mell pace alternated every other day with a six-mile jog slow enough to make conversation easy.

What Parker predicted came true in just a few weeks. I was building an aerobic base on my easy days, while strengthening the heart and building speed on hard days. On a particularly cool, dry day in late January, I tried a hard six-mile run to prepare for an upcoming 10K race and found myself finishing so much earlier than usual that I could be seen in my driveway tapping my stopwatch to see if it still worked.

The training isn't possible without a heart rate monitor. The average runner is typically trying to match a time on a particular training route. But, as Parker says, the heart monitor doesn't lie. It knows when you have a cold, when you've been on a poor diet, when the humidity is a dripping 90%, when you've been stressed out or haven't slept well. Your heart works harder in those situations, and the monitor tells you when to speed up or slow down. Look at your monitor, not your watch.

So wedded did I become to my monitor that I even wore it in weekend races. I'd learned I could run a 10K and maintain my best steady pace with a heart rate of about 165 or about 90% of my actual maximum.

Above 170 was in the red zone—it meant I was overheating and needed to slow down a bit. I kept an eye on this unerring heart gauge and knocked down all my race times in just seven weeks.

There's more to the heart rate monitor than race times, though.

Since strapping on the monitor, the number I'm proudest of is 47. That's my resting heart beat, well below the 60 to 70 that's average. Forty-seven is a strong indicator that my heart is strong and healthy. And health, after all, is the reason I run.

Update:

I continue to be a discliple, and in fact have indoctrinated several people in my office, one of whom I expect to beat me handily in a few weeks at the New York City Marathon.

After turning 50 this year, as you might expect, I've lost a few steps in the 5K and 10K, but my emphasis has been turning more toward the triathlon. I do seven or eight of them a summer, and this past summer was delighted to post a five minute PR in the St. Anthony's Tampa Bay Olympic-distance event in about three hours flat.

I was recently working out on a treadmill at my gym and someone asked me about the monitor as I was getting off the machine. Before I realized it, I had pretty much given her a complete heart monitor training seminar!

Proselytizing like that at the drop of a hat must be the sign of a True Believer.

October, 1999

The Show Runner

by Reid Vannoy

(The author is a soon-to-be masters runner and a management consultant at the Florida Center for Public Management at Florida State University in Tallahassee, Florida.)

I was a decent enough runner at a small Indiana high school with pathetic coaching. But I progressed well enough to record a 4:40 mile and 10:20 two-mile by my senior year and a love of competitive running was permanently instilled in me. College running at Miami of Ohio University, however, was way too intimidating, and I settled into road racing.

In the 1980s my training buddy Dale and I used to call ourselves "show runners" because the few (20 to 25) miles we ran every week were almost all fast. I must have had some natural ability, because I seemed to get by with this and even do reasonably well in races. On quality alone I would beat people who ran many more miles in training.

I consistently ran 10K's in the high 32's to low 33's and 5K's in the low 16's. I even attempted some longer races and was successful up to the half-marathon. I recall a Virginia 10-miler time of 54:40 and a Citrus Bowl half marathon of 74:00. My approach was to run five days a week with one interval workout and one longer workout.

I ran most workouts as fast as I could tolerate. This usually involved getting into oxygen debt quickly and staying there the whole workout. After a day off my runs went great. Running a second day in a row was usually a bummer. Races were usually preceded by one day of complete rest (sometimes two!) just so I could feel recovered enough to race. Like I said, this was generally fun because my racing was successful and the investment in training time was moderate. (And just so you know, I don't run because it is necessarily "fun." If I was looking for a fun sport I would take up croquet or snow skiing or something. I also don't run because of the relaxed feeling that follows—although I'll have to admit it's pretty neat. I run to get fast, kick butt, and thump my chest when I do well. I apologize in advance if some find that offensive.)

Well, my running enjoyment came to an abrupt end in 1990 when I was 32.

I had taken a six-month hiatus to start graduate school, but then started training again, thinking to make my mark on a new running scene. Employing my sure-fire approach to getting into racing shape fast, I soon found myself grounded with strained calf muscles. The problem would not go away, so I quit training altogether. Over the course of the next seven years, seven similar comeback efforts ended the same way, with the same injury. I spent a lot of time with a different hobby, gained some weight, and read the local racing results enviously, wishing the hot shots were eating my dust.

But I do have some common sense, though sometimes it takes a while to kick in. A year ago I began another training campaign. I mean, I was only 38. Didn't I remember some 40-year old guy winning a major marathon years back in 2:14? I thought, I can't be too old to compete. I must be doing something wrong. So I forced myself into some new rules. I started out running mostly flat soft surfaces because I figured that pavement and pounding downhills were aggravating my calves. (I later found out that this was true and that I was suffering from a malady someone calls "Calf Heart

Attacks," but that's another story.) And I ran slowly for months to see if I could strengthen all those leg muscles before I asked them to do speed work. This went pretty well for a while, though I kind of hit a barrier that kept me from running more than four or five times a week, rarely exceeding 20 miles in a single week. In addition, I wouldn't risk a sustained pace much quicker than 7:00 per mile. Fast paces left my calves feeling like they would relapse, and if that happened the comeback would be over.

Then, by stroke of luck, I met a famous running guy who had been helping people run better for years. It happened like this: One day I was considering entering the trail system of the Apalachicola National Forest and wondering how long it would take someone to find my decomposed body if I got lost. John L. Parker, who was also getting ready to run, volunteered to be my guide. He was wearing this contraption around his chest that looked like it was designed to either facilitate husband leashing or sadistically restrict one's lung capacity. He was also running slow, really slow. I mean, I thought I could walk faster. I didn't say anything critical to him though, for fear I might wake him out of his running slumber.

But I enjoyed the pine needle-covered trail and we started meeting regularly to run. For a while I was just happy to have found a terrific trail and a partner to plod it with, so running slowly didn't bother me much.

And I found out that Parker didn't run snail-like every day. Some days he ran faster "tempo" runs and other days he ran intervals, all right there on the trail. But the slow "recovery" runs were a regular ingredient in the mix. Well, running seven miles at a slow pace leaves a lot of time for talking, and not knowing the way around the trail well enough to navigate it myself, I was pretty much a

captive audience. I learned a lot about heart monitor training.

Finally one day I strapped on one of the devices.
Actually Parker strapped it on me. He didn't even
ask permission. Using it a couple times a week on
recovery runs, setting it to a best guess rate of 130
beats per minute for my 70% "ceiling," I almost
immediately found that I could add another running
day per week to my schedule without feeling that I
was on the verge of injury. It took some time to
develop patience and stifle the urge to go fast, but
soon I started to enjoy the recovery runs like one
enjoys a walk in the park. If I got antsy, I told
myself, I could go fast the next day.

Over the course of several months, we had to
adjust my training chart because we kept finding
out my max was higher than we previously thought
(it went from 178 to 180 to 185 to, finally, 190,
which I saw at the end of a 5K race). Thus my 70%
recovery rate turned out to be about 140, my 80-
85% tempo rate about 160-168, and my 90% intervals about 175.

The changes in my program might seem subtle
to some people. Before starting the heart monitor
program, I was running only four or five days a
week, thinking any more mileage might invite
injury. John suggested that instead of taking days
completely off, I might run at recovery pace on
those days. That way I could increase my mileage
while still taking it easy on my calves. And instead
of running what amounted to quick tempo runs
whenever I felt like it, I now ran fast only every
other day or so. Even weekly intervals are allowed
as long as they are followed by recovery days.

It was only about six weeks ago that I started
the program so I think I am still in the very early
stages, but even in this short amount of time I have
had encouraging results.

Keep in mind that my objectives at the time were to increase my mileage, run effective speed work, and eventually race. I already had done some consistent training when I started the monitor program, so I wasn't starting strictly from scratch. At any rate, after less than two months on the program, here's what we've seen so far:

• Before I started monitor training, I was running an average of 17-20 miles a week. Now I run 35-40 miles a week. I've added two recovery training days a week, which means at least 15 more miles in my running week with few detrimental effects and a lot of cool results, like dropping some unwanted weight and building more endurance.

• My "long" training run used to be seven miles. Now I can run 11 miles comfortably. Through the longer "monitored" recovery runs, I have proven to myself that my legs can still endure distance. Even my tempo runs have gotten longer. This might not have been possible were it not for the rigid pace enforcement of the monitor.

• Before, my tempo pace was about 7:10 per mile. Now it's 6:40. I now firmly believe that it takes more miles to yield faster miles if you want to stay uninjured and you don't want to suffer the roller coaster effects of exhaustion/elation. It's kind of counterintuitive that adding slow miles will eventually help you run fast but I think I am seeing the proof.

• Even my recovery run pace is getting faster. A recovery run that a month ago would have taken 1:02 regulated at 140 beats per minute now takes two or three minutes less. I think that will continue to drop as I get into better shape.

• I'm apparently successfully avoiding injury, which means I can stride out without all my old fears of muscle strains, tears, and other bad and painful things.

• Last and not least, my racing results have been consistently encouraging. A few weeks after starting heart monitor training I decided to run a time trial to test my progress. I picked 5K as the distance, and at Parker's suggestion, wore the monitor to help pace myself (since I hadn't raced in eight years!). With mile splits of 5:40, 6:05, and 6:00 and a final time of 18:12, I was elated. That was almost a minute better than I was hoping. The program was working.

Several 40-mile weeks later, I finished my first race, a muggy, hilly 10K, in 38:19 (again, wearing the monitor to regulate the early miles so I could finish strong). I was in the top 50 overall, and won prize money in my age group!

Several weeks after that, at a small 5K nearby, I finished under 18:00 and second overall. And this past weekend, in a local 5K, I cruised to a 17:42 5K and was third overall.

Now these results are a far cry from the 16's and the 34's of 10 years ago, but then again I'm kind of an old guy now.

I may not be a "show runner" any more, but I'm not the non-runner my previous training was turning me into, either. And I'm still in the early stages of this program: I think I can race a good bit faster.

And maybe the best part of this story is that I'm having fun running again.

Update:

Update? Well, okay. I'm now 41, I still run the trails around Tallahassee to the tune of about 35 miles each week. I race nearly every other weekend during the fall and winter season and have developed an affinity for cross country races (as good an excuse as any for not performing well on the roads).

My masters PRs of 36:40 for 10K and 17:40 for 5K could fall this racing season barring any training interruptions (achilles strain, calf micro-tears, and possibly even snakebite). I continue to follow the intent if not the letter of Heart Monitor Training, using a delicate mix of recovery runs, tempo runs, and intervals to leverage my moderate mileage and thwart injury.

I recently added a weekly long—for me—run of 10-11 miles in hopes of improving endurance. My most humbling recent racing experience was a 20K trail race through the hilly forests of the North Florida Panhandle. I finished in 1:27, which is not as bad as it sounds. The course was such a bear that that time got me in the top 10 overall and second in my age group. Immediate post-race quote: "I never would have thought I could be so satisfied with seven-minute miles."

October, 1999

12. Racing with a Monitor

Someone I know, a 15:00 5K masters runner, won't wear a monitor in a race because he feels it's an unethical advantage. I agree that it can be a definite help, particularly for an inexperienced racer, but he has yet to explain to me why it's perfectly okay to use such an unfair advantage in training but not in racing. It would be as if a sprinter like Ben Johnson said, "Okay, I won't take steroids *on the day of the race.*"

Is racing with a monitor ethical?

Anyway, when you stop to consider how efficient it is to run an evenly *paced* race, imagine how efficient it would be if you could run a race at even *effort!* That's precisely what a heart monitor allows you to do. Imagine the advantage a first-time marathoner can gain by wearing a monitor and avoiding the dreaded wall by running the first 15 to 20 miles at a sane pace. Or a 5K runner going out at in a very fast first mile, but with perfect confidence that the pace is in line with his conditioning and thus he won't accidentally be sliding into oxygen debt before mile two.

The figures below are very general. Physiological research is starting to show very clearly that not only do athletes reach their anaerobic thresholds at

Anaerobic threshold varies greatly in individuals

different points, but that athletes differ in their abilities to hold different effort levels over a period of time.[1] Which makes perfect sense. World class marathoners are able to operate at 85-90% of max over the course of an entire marathon, whereas we mere mortals would dry up and blow away by the halfway mark. Clearly, one of the benefits of high-level fitness is the ability to sustain very high levels of effort for much longer periods of time than lesser training allows.

So these figures come with a caveat. Wear your monitor in all phases of training. Get to know your own heart monitor "numbers" like you know your telephone number. You will soon be able to determine precisely what your most efficient effort level is for most racing distances. Once you know those numbers, simply wear your monitor in races and use enough discipline to keep your head when all about you are losing theirs.

The general effort levels for racing

General HR Maximal Effort Levels for Standard Racing Distances:	
one mile:	98-100%
5K	90%
10K	85%
half-marathon	80%
marathon	75%

One further caveat: I often advise first-time marathoners to stay under 70% for the first 20 miles. That's conservative, but it almost assures a completed race and a happy first-timer rather than one of those Death Marches we've all heard about (or experienced). Besides, if you make it to 20 and feel like Yobes Ondieki, go ahead and sprint in! Just think how great you'll look in your finish line photo!

A personal experience in the marathon

I have experimented with using a monitor in races of varying distances, and have found it to be particularly useful in the marathon.

In the 1995 Twin Cities event, I used a heart monitor in the first marathon I had run in over 20 years. I needed a qualifying time for the 100th Boston, and I was convinced the monitor could help me get one with as little wear and tear as possible. Here is the report, pretty much as I wrote about it for *Running Times*:[2]

My plan was to run strictly on my heart monitor at 75% of my max heart rate for 20 miles, and then if my legs hadn't turned to beef jerky, to go hard the last 10K. I had only been training consistently for six weeks, and had done no runs longer than 12 miles, but I had been getting in good weekly mileage (50-80), and felt I could finish well, so long as I kept the early pace well under control.

The monitor keeps me on track

I made the mistake of starting the race with Scott Samuelson and a friend of his. Scott is Joanie Benoit Samuelson's lanky, good-natured husband, and because all good Mainers stick together, his home state friend had agreed to pace Scott to his own Boston qualifying time, as well as a possible PR. Optimism was running high on a beautiful 40-degree October day.

Within a half-mile of the start I was up to 85%. I told Scott and his buddy so long. A few minutes later, they were joined by Joanie, who was doing the first 17 miles as a training run and to help "pace" Scott. Her idea of pacing is to "run how you feel," which is perfectly fine if you "feel" like running 2:21:21, which she has. Scott, on the other hand, would have probably been better off just taking a ball peen hammer to his kneecaps.

Altering my plan in mid-race

Anyway, I didn't exactly stick to my plan either. It was a perfect day for marathoning, and it felt so darned easy, after Scott and his friend ran on off and left me I decided to compromise with myself and run at 80% of my max (around 160). Occasionally I found myself edging up over that number, but for the most part I exercised uncommon good discipline and kept reining in my pace until I was near my mark. I ran much of the mileage at around 163 or so. It was remarkable how dead even the splits were.

Still feeling great until mile 17

All the way through 10, 12, 15 miles I felt terrific. Right around 17 or so, something changed. I began to realize the wisdom of this conservative plan. It wasn't as if I fell apart, but all of a sudden I could definitely feel that I had run a long way.

Still, I stuck with the program. When at long last I hit 20, I didn't feel fresh as a daisy, as it had seemed earlier that I would. But, all in all, I had to admit that I didn't feel as bad as I had in my first and only marathon 20 years earlier.

Raising my HR to 85-90% over the last 6 miles

I picked up my effort to 85-90% over the last six miles, but all it did was keep me on pace. Other than a few seconds of truly terrifying cramps in my quads at around mile 22, the end of the race went remarkably smoothly, though I shuddered to think what it would have been like had I given in to temptation and run even harder than 80% in the early miles. It wasn't long before the reality of such folly presented itself to me.

Reuniting with Scott and his friend

About a half-mile from the finish, I roared by Scott and his friend so fast I didn't see them. As I circled back to run with them for a ways, I could tell immediately they were in a survival mode. Scott had already had to stop and walk several times with severe cramps in his calves. He looked decidedly unwell. His buddy's brow was wrinkled in helpless empathy for his friend. Joanie had long since left the scene, leaving Scott's poor friend to try to pick up the pieces. After a few minutes of trying to make encouraging noises, I excused myself and sprinted in, truly awed by how painless the heart monitor had made the marathon experience.

Well within semi-geezer qualifying with my 3:08:15, I was relieved to see Scott and his friend finishing a half a minute or so later. Although it felt like someone had taken an ice-pick to my quads, otherwise I had to admit I felt pretty darned good.

When last I saw them, Scott and his friend were having a pretty earnest discussion about heart monitors.

Boston: a slightly different story

Interestingly enough, six months later when I used a monitor to run Boston, despite being in considerably better shape, I came very close to finishing in my own death march.

But it wasn't the monitor's fault. Far from it.

Maybe it was Boston's famous crowds, maybe it was those early downhill miles, whatever the reason I somehow managed to talk myself into the proposition that because I was in so much better shape, I could sustain a higher percentage of max to mile 20 and still finish strongly.

Just four or five beats difference can spell disaster

Here's the instructive part: I'm not talking about a large difference in heart rates, just five beats or so. But what a difference!

I ran the first half of Boston with a heart rate of around 167 or 168. How I could convince myself that this was a reasonable strategy, I really cannot fathom.

At the halfway point, I was on pace for a 2:50 marathon! And I actually felt okay, at least for another mile or two. Then I really began to feel it:

those sharp, stabbing pains in the top of the quads, as the muscle fibers begin to tear from the pounding; the queasy ketosis in the belly of the calves and quads that warn of imminent cramping.

Shifting to survival mode just in time

But at least I had sense enough to immediately shift to survival mode, which is what saved the day. I was deteriorating from mile 15 on, but I respected what the monitor was telling me, and backed off to what truly felt like a jog. I had run the final eight miles with a suffering friend the year before, and I knew all too well what a difference there was between being able to run at all, and not. And I was determined to avoid the agony of the forced jog/walk to the finish.

The wisdom of this strategy was born out by the legions of the Walking Undead in the last three miles of that race.

Three hours was within reach, but just barely

But so close had I come to the abyss that when I got to the "one mile to go" marker, the time was exactly 2:52, and I can clearly remember the awful realization that I really didn't know if I could run an eight-minute mile to get under three hours.

I did, but not by much. And the race left me a proverbial basket case for many days, with all that entails—backing down stairs, easing into chairs with an undignified yelp—the whole thing.

I had tried to deviate from the iron law of the heart monitor and had nearly paid a very high price. Fortunately, I wised up in time to salvage the situation, but it could have easily gone the other way.

Word to the wise.

You know you're a runner when you . . .

. . . never stop for cars.

13. Putting It All Together: Adapting the Monitor to Your Own Training

You're basically there. If you've read and generally understood everything in the preceding chapters, you should be able to adapt heart monitoring to your own training program, whether you're an elite runner on a sophisticated marathon program, or a back-of-the-packer who doesn't want to get into anything too complicated.

Do you "just run?"

Let's take a simple case first. What if you're one of these folks who goes out there and "just runs?" Say, for instance, you "just run" six miles a day. You've been doing it for a while, and you've gotten in reasonably good shape. Everyone in your office or neighborhood or club is impressed, but you've hit a plateau and you want to start making some appearances on the stage at awards time.

Building in the Yin and Yang

Here's the general strategy: Start building some yin and yang into your training. First, build a "hard" day or two into your program.

Do it like this: After at least two 70% recovery days, go out and run your first two miles at below your Recovery Ceiling. Call it a warm up. Stop and do some stretching if you want, but don't lollygag around. Then do the last four miles at 80-85% of your max, a real tempo run.

Then the next day, your recovery day, make sure you stay below 70%. Do at least two recovery days in a row before trying another "hard" day.

After a week or so, as you get stronger, instead of staying with the same mileage, add a mile or two to your recovery run. The general idea is: a little shorter and faster on hard days, a little longer and slower on easy days.

This method can work for any level of runner

Runners at just about any ability level can apply the same principle to their training with good results. You might be a talented post-collegiate runner doing an eight-mile tempo run at 5:30 pace. Or you might be a decent age-grouper doing three miles at 7:10. You might be a total beginner doing a single mile at 8:30. The key thing is that they're all running at 85% of max, and they're all recovering well because of their 70% recovery days. And they're all raring to go on their next hard day!

When it comes to hard days, as I've said before, I'm not too worried about the specifics. Many coaches think of themselves as geniuses at whipping out complicated interval workout programs or fartlek scenarios, and I hate to be a party-pooper, but in real life the truth is plain and boring: It's the easiest thing in the world to sit down and write out a hard interval workout.

Hard days usually take care of them-selves

But in this program, hard days tend to take care of themselves. Runners like to run fast. It's the icing on the cake.

It's the so-called "easy" days that torpedo otherwise good training plans. And you don't have to err by much to blow it. On a regular basis, five or 10% over your 70% Recovery Ceiling is enough to do it. A heart monitor will keep you from making that all-too-typical mistake, and give you a leg up on most of your fellow runners who think they "know their own bodies" well enough to judge the correct pace subjectively.

A Simple Example

Adjusting a typical runner's schedule

Let's take a typical case of Tim Simple, a runner who basically runs six miles a day, six days a week. Assuming this runner takes Sunday off, how would you apply heart monitor training to Tim's training?

Since Sunday is his day off, start off with a 70% 8-mile run on Monday to give him two recovery days in a row. As Tim improves with the program, we'll think about increasing the length of this run to 10 miles, possibly even 12.

Now he's had two easy days in a row. On Tuesday, he's due for a hard day, so let's schedule a tempo run. But instead of telling him to run six miles at 85% of his max, we'll specify that he do 2 easy miles (60-65%) as a warm-up, a 3-mile tempo run at 85-90%, then a 1-mile easy run (60-65%) as a cooldown. Notice that on his hard day Tim is running the same mileage as before, but half of the total workout is done at an easy pace.

Wednesday and Thursday are 70% days like Monday. For variation, we might specify that Wednesday is only six miles (to aid in recovery from Tuesday's hard run) and Thursday is 8 miles.

Friday will be another tempo run like Tuesday, or possibly an interval workout, something like 4 X 800 meters at 85-90% of max.

Adjusting for races or for long runs

Saturday would be another 70% day. If Tim is racing on Saturday, he would adjust his schedule so that Friday was a 70% day, and race day on Saturday would count as his hard day. If Tim were training for a marathon and doing a long run on the weekend, then he would adjust his schedule so that he had a 70% day before his long run, which he would count as a hard day (even though he should be doing most of that run at 70-75% of max). Here's an overview of how a monitor might change.

Tim's typical week:

Tim Simple, Typical Training Week
BEFORE Using HM

Mon   6 miles @ 80-85% of max
Tue   6 miles @ 80-85% of max
Wed   6 miles @ 80-85% of max
Thu   6 miles @ 80-85% of max
Fri   6 miles @ 80-85% of max
Sat   6 miles @ 80-85% of max
Sun   Off
Total mileage: 36
Total number of "hard" days: 6

Tim Simple, Typical Training Week
AFTER Using HM

Mon   8 miles @ 70% of max
Tue   3 m. tempo run @ 85% of max
        + 3 m. warm-up & cooldown
Wed   6 miles @ 70% of max
Thu   8 miles @ 70% of max
Fri   3 m. tempo run @ 85% of
        max + 3 m. warm-up & cooldown
Sat   6 miles @ 70% of max
Sun   Off
Total mileage: 40
Total number of "hard" days: 2

I wouldn't recommend that Tim make a lot of changes to his regimen at one time. He might, for instance, keep his Sunday off for a few weeks, to make sure his body is adapting to the changes, then add an easy Sunday run. Or he might not increase the length of his 70% recovery runs right away, keeping them at six miles for a few weeks, just to see how he feels.

Rapid increases in training are possible

On the other hand, I've found that many runners get such immediate benefit from their 70% days that they are able to rapidly implement these other changes, and still have fewer injuries and feel more rested and energetic between workouts.

But note the counterintuitive nature of what I'm saying here: Using this approach this typical runner *can run an additional 10 or more miles a week,* and still be better rested, risk fewer injuries, and get in much better racing shape.

Running more but risking less

A More Complicated Case

Let's take someone like Gail Goodtrophy, a semi-elite runner on a sophisticated training regimen that involves one long run, one interval workout, one tempo run, and four recovery days each week.

Hammerheads are tougher cases

Because her program is already built around the hard/easy principle (at least in theory), the best use of a heart monitor in such a program would be simply to insure that the recovery days are truly under 70%, that her hard days are getting her into the appropriate ranges, and that her long run is in the 70 to 75% range. By doing so, she'll be able to increase the mileage of her recovery days right away, and later she may also want to go a few miles longer on her long run.

But because she is training on a more sophisticated level than Tim Simple, Gail can really get a good deal more use out of the monitor on the high

*The moni-
tor can be
even
more
valuable
for these
runners*

end. By wearing her monitor on tempo and interval days and checking her heart rate from time to time in order to keep track of what kind of effort she is putting into these more intense efforts.

As she gets in better shape and attempts to peak for a big race, she'll be sure that her intervals and tempo runs get up in the 85-95% range, or even higher. In fact, as she gets closer to an all out peak, her intervals will get shorter, and her efforts will sometimes be at 95 to 100% of max.

Lets look at how two of Gail's typical weeks might vary before and after using a heart monitor.

Gail Goodtrophy, Typical Week BEFORE Using HM

Mon	8 miles @ 80% of max
Tue	6 mile tempo @ 90% of max
Wed	8 miles @ 80-85% of max
Thu	intervals, 10 X 400M @ 90-95%
Fri	8 miles @ 80% of max
Sat	8 miles @ 80% of max
Sun	15 miles @ 75-80% of max

Total mileage: 59
Total number of "hard" days: 7

Gail Goodtrophy, Typical Week
AFTER Using HM

Mon	10 miles @ 70% of max
Tue	4 mile tempo @ 85-90% of max
	(with 2m warm-up and 2m cooldown)
Wed	10 miles @ 70% of max
Thu	10 X 400M @ 90-95%
	(with 2m warm-up, 1m striders,
	1m cooldown)
Fri	8 miles @ 70% of max
Sat	10 miles @ 70% of max
Sun	17 miles @ 70-75% of max

Total mileage: 72
Total number of "hard" days: 3

The new program is actually much easier on her

Many runners would look at this comparison and predict doom for Gail. You can't increase an already ambitious mileage goal by 22%, they'd say, and not expect injuries or breakdown or both.

But most runners would be basing that judgment on what would happen if they implemented such an increase in their own program. And that would simply mean adding another 13 miles at the pace at which they already run most of their training, which is 80-85% (in which case, I would agree with them, by the way).

In fact, though, Gail's "After" training is physically much easier on her despite her running an additional 13 miles during the week. The key is the difference in the number of hard days. In the "After" scenario, she'll recover properly after her hard days and will be ready to go again when the schedule calls for it.

In her "Before" schedule, she's barely hanging

on from day to day. Like Sally Strideasy we discussed earlier in the book, despite the fact that Gail's program is much more varied and sophisticated, sooner or later she's going to get injured or crash.

On the other hand, if she sticks to the "After" program, she'll get stronger from week to week, with her interval and tempo times coming down and perhaps even adding a mile or two to her recovery days and her long run.

The long run counts as a hard day

Incidentally, the reason I count the weekly long run as a hard day, even though a lot of it is run at 70-75% of max, is that you're still burning up a lot of glycogen in the workout. It's the distance that burns it up, not the intensity, but the result is the same.

Remember, your ability to come back the next day and handle another training session depends mostly on whether you've used up your glycogen supply in previous workouts.

Therefore, to my way of thinking:

High Glycogen Use = Hard Day

Low Glycogen Use = Easy Day

Adjusting Your Own Program

Now to put this all together for your own program. Let's say you're one of these folks like Tim Simple who goes out there and "just runs." Perhaps, like Tim, you run about six miles a day, with a day or two off each week. You've been doing it for a while, and you've gotten in reasonably good shape. Everyone in your office or neighborhood or club is impressed, but you've hit a plateau and you want to start making some appearances on the stage at awards time.

As I did with Tim's new schedule, I would propose that you start building some yin and yang into your training. After two true 70% days, go out for your hard day and run your first two miles at below your Recovery Ceiling. Call it a warm up. Stop and do some stretching if you want, but don't lollygag around. Then do the last four miles at 80-90% of your max, a real tempo run.

Then the next day, your recovery day, make sure you stay below 70%. After a week or so, as you get stronger, instead of just trying to run your hard day faster, add a mile or two to your recovery run. The general idea is: a little shorter and faster on hard days, a little longer and slower on easy days.

It doesn't really matter what level of runner you are. The more competitive you are, the more important it is that your intervals and tempo runs are designed to be challenging enough, yet not so tough as to lead to overtraining.

"Listening to your body" may be a big mistake

A heart monitor can keep you from making that all-too-common mistake, and give you a leg up on most of your fellow runners who think they "know their own bodies" well enough to judge the correct pace subjectively.

If you're ready to abandon your old training ideas altogether and you want to adopt a ready-made heart monitor training program whole cloth, the next chapter sets out three-month programs tailored to four different level of runner.

14. An All-Purpose 12-Week Training Plan for Runners

The training schedules below are meant to be used as a general guide for a runner aiming to run a serious race effort at the end of 12 weeks. The workouts are meant to conservatively build in intensity and/or duration week by week until the final week, at which point all efforts are geared towards rest and intensity; in short, peaking.

Flexibility

As with all such programs, the individual runner must approach the plan with some flexibility. First, you should be flexible as to the level you decide you belong in. A 23:00 5K runner might conceivably fall into either the intermediate or the advanced category. The weekly mileage comparisons is the primary consideration in selecting the right one. The 5K and 10K PRs are primarily listed for runners who have raced in the past but are not doing much current training.

All of the schedules set forth below will eventually exceed the mileage estimates in the Selection Chart, which, after all, is one of the true goals and benefits of heart monitor training.

119

*Be
flexible in
your
choice of
levels*

You may need to change categories after a week or two. The mileage may be too much, or the number and/or intensity of the intervals may convince you to drop back a level. Alternatively, you may find your original selection ridiculously easy to maintain and decide you're made of much sterner stuff. I'd give it at least two weeks before upgrading yourself. The schedules are meant to start off gently, but ratchet up in difficulty quickly. Using the monitor to enforce true 70% days often convinces the new user that he or she is handling the training very easily, when in fact the increased mileage will quickly catch up with the athlete.

Selection Chart–Choose Your Level

(use weekly mileage unless you're a veteran runner starting from scratch)

	Weekly Mileage	5K PR	10K PR
Novice	10-20	25:00-30:00	55:00-65:00
Intermediate	20-30	23:00- 25:00	50:00-55:00
Advanced	30-40	20:00-23:00	45:00-50:00
Competitive	40-50	18:00-20:00	38:00-45:00

Where to Start

I assume that the runner is already in decent shape and ready for real training. You may not be capable of the PRs assigned for your chosen level, but you should be doing weekly mileage in the given range for your group; for example, if you have placed yourself as an Intermediate, you should be generally be already running 20-30 miles per week.

You may need to "get in shape to train" first

If that's not the case, if you are starting strictly from scratch (perhaps coming off a long layoff or illness), then you probably need to "get in shape to train." Appendix C, starting on page 231, sets out a 30-day "Starting from Scratch" program for each ability level. I recommend that even accomplished runners begin with this program if they haven't been training regularly for a month or more. You may find you only need two weeks of the "comeback" training before you start on the 12-week program, but you'll be avoiding the setbacks and potential injury problems likely to befall the eager beavers who jump right into the full-blown 12-week schedule.

Adjusting to Reality

Often it is impossible to make real life conform to some idealistic, predetermined schedule. What if you're scheduled for a sub-70% six-miler and an old running friend comes to town and you just can't resist going out for a run? Then say the "easy" run turns into a hard 10-miler? Well, obviously you don't want to be deviating drastically from the plan all the time, otherwise why have a plan at all? On the other hand, it's not meant to be a strait jacket.

"Flexible discipline" is the key

You just need to use common sense. If your unscheduled hard 10-miler falls on a scheduled "easy" day, you certainly don't want to go out the next day and "Get back in sync" by doing a hard interval workout just because the schedule calls for it. Go ahead and count the 10-miler as a hard tempo run, then fill in your schedule with recovery runs at your usual distance until the following hard day.

Days Off

Common sense and the long distance runner

If you're accustomed to taking one or more days for cross training or completely off, go ahead and substitute them for recovery days. Days off are built into the schedules for the Novice and Intermediate levels. I would suggest, however, that for the more competitive levels, taking more than two days a week completely off will render the 12-week program (or any serious training plan, for that matter) much less effective. However, you've got to be a student of your own body and decide how well it adapts to the stress of training. Many runners will thrive on seven-day-per-week training. Others, including some very good runners, will need one or two days a week of complete rest.

Give Yourself a Break Today

People are not machines

On the other hand, even seven-day-per-week trainers should be flexible enough to deal on an ad hoc basis with normal human ups and down, biorythms, or what have you. We're not machines and there are a lot of complicated processes going on simultaneously in the human body. This training plan is not an attempt to over-ride mother nature. If you are scheduled for a hard day and you feel like hell, bag it! Give yourself another recovery day, or even a day off if you need it. If you feel like it the next day, you can do the hard workout then, or you can simply skip it altogether that week.

A heart monitor can give you wonderful insight into how you're recovering from your training. Use it to get a resting heart rate in the mornings, or wear it occasionally during your work day. If you're scheduled for a hard training session, but discover that you're consistently 10-15 beats higher than normal, listen to your body! Take another easy day. Back off and live to fight another day. It's not wimpiness or cowardice, it's just being smart.

Using the monitor during the day

Runners who don't use such discretion may get reputations for toughness or consistency, but they are also often laid up with injuries or flu bugs when everyone else is still training. There's nothing less efficient in a training program than an involuntary layoff for weeks or months because of illness or injury.

Consistency

The flip side of flexibility is discipline and consistency

Now for the flip side of the foregoing. The most successful athletes are the ones who are most consistent in training. You have to use your best judgment, of course, but don't just blow off your workouts whenever you feel like it. You really do need to apply a lot of discipline to excel in endurance sports, and that means on occasion going out to train when it may not be your number one favorite thing to be doing at the moment. Indeed, I've occasionally found that days when I felt lethargic and lazy have turned out to be some of my best training days ever. (They've sometimes been my worst, too.) You can't tell from superficial subjective feelings during the day how you're going to feel halfway through the workout. Somewhere along the way, I came up with "the Two-Mile Rule," which states that you shouldn't try to decide how you feel on any given day until after the first two miles of your workout. At that point, if I still feel awful, I'll bag the whole thing. Often, though, by that point in the run, I've completely forgotten that I didn't even feel like lacing up my shoes on that day.

The "Two-Mile Rule"

So skipping or truncating a workout shouldn't be a matter of whim. You should do it only when you have a good reason for doing so.

One of the great benefits of training with a heart monitor is that if you follow it closely, you should generally be well-rested and eager to train from day to day. If not, if you find yourself dragging, barely making the schedule at all, then something's surely wrong. Either you've overmatched yourself in your category, you've got a physical problem of some kind, or possibly the max or resting numbers you're working with are off.

If you're dragging, something's wrong

Failing that, the day-to-day training should be challenging but "doable," a livable schedule that you don't think of as some kind of athletic torture.

Interim Racing

Few runners, once they start getting in shape, can resist hopping into the local Kentucky Fried Chicken 5K and Egg Roll.

It's only natural to want to test your progress and strut your stuff.

Racing is not to be taken lightly

But you'll notice there is only one race on the schedule, and there's a good reason for that: Racing and hard training go together like oil and water. The really good runners know that and they try to avoid hard racing when they're doing hard training. Getting ready to race requires more rest, it requires sharper intervals, it requires fewer miles. In short, it interferes with truly serious training.

Does that mean you shouldn't run any races at all? Well, if you just can't help yourself, here's what I suggest. First, don't race at all for *at least* the first four weeks. After that, I certainly wouldn't race more often than every third week, and even then I would do what the good runners do, which is to "run through" the race. What does that mean? It

Running "through" a race: it's what the good guys do

means you don't take the race very seriously. You do your training pretty much as normal right up to race day. Of course, you don't do a hard workout the day before your race, but you might well do your standard recovery run. You might also cut your mileage back slightly the day before the race, but certainly make no more concessions than that.

Then you treat the race as a tempo run, and you try not to get all wrapped up in your performance. Remember, you're *running through* the race, so you're not supposed to expect much. You should really treat it like a glorified workout. Wear the monitor, run under control, and keep your ego in check. If your friends make sarcastic comments about your "high tech gadget" training program, just smile and say, "Oh, I'm just 'running through.'" If they're knowledgeable, they'll be impressed. If not, they'll be confused. In any case, the real object is to keep your powder dry until your target race at the end of the 12th week.

So, in short, don't race at all during the 12-week buildup if you can possibly help it. If you must, run something shorter than a 10K and then practice "running through" it.

The Long Term

While this is a 12-week schedule, it would be easy to expand it 16, 20, 24 weeks or so. Simply take the training of the 9th or 10th week and maintain that level, occasionally adding some intensity and/or mileage when it feels comfortable to do so.

However, trying to maintain a steady increase in training intensity and bulk over a much longer period of time is a mistake. Good coaches know that athletes need "fallow" periods, "base building" periods, and so on. You do not get good results by simply increasing the work load until you make the Olympic team. What happens is that you increase

Thinking about periodizing your training

the work load until you break. This whole subject area is known to physiologists and coaches as "periodicity" and is too complex a concept to build into a 12-week program. Runners and coaches who want to know more about the subject should turn to Appendix B on page 217 and read my article on the subject.

All right, that's it. That's all the quibbles, warnings, and disclaimers I can think of. Now it's time to pick your ability level (see the box on page 120), strap on your monitor, and get to it!

Workout Notations

<   "less than," or under a specified effort. "<70%" means "less than 70% of Max HR."

m   meters; "400m" is 400 meters.

@   "at" a specified pace or effort level. Example: "400m @ 85%" would indicate a 400 meter repeat run at 85% of Max HR.

striders   100 meter repeats at near sprint speed, but under control and with good running form. Always start easily and build up speed for 20 meters, run fast but controlled for 60 meters, then coast to a jog for 20 meters. Striders are usually run hard/easy, ie. 100 meters hard, then 100 meters at a jog to recover. They are often run back and forth on a grass field or on the outside lanes of a track, and are usually done before races or hard interval workouts.

X   "times"; 4 X 400m means 4 repeats of 400 meters.

w/   "with"; indicates a specified recovery. "w/ 200m jog" indicates a recovery of 200 meters between the interval repeats.

12 Week Program—Novice—Week 1

		Total Miles
Monday	3 Miles <70%	3
Tuesday	5 Miles <70%	5
Wednesday	OFF	0
Thursday	1 Mile jog <65%; 1 Mile @ 80%; 1 Mile jog <65%	3
Friday	3 Miles <70%	3
Saturday	3 Miles <70%	3
Sunday	Off	0

Weekly Mileage   17
Hard Days   1

12 Week Program—Novice—Week 2

Novice Level:

WEEK 2

		Total Miles
Monday	3 Miles <70%	3
Tuesday	5 Miles <70%	5
Wednesday	OFF	0
Thursday	1 Mile jog <65%; 1 Mile @ 80%; 1 Mile jog <65%	3
Friday	3 Miles <70%	3
Saturday	5 Miles <70%	5
Sunday	Off	0

Weekly Mileage	19
Hard Days	1

12 Week Program—Novice—Week 3

Novice Level:

WEEK 3

		Total Miles
Monday	3 Miles <70%	3
Tuesday	5 Miles <70%	5
Wednesday	OFF	0
Thursday	1 Mile jog <65%; 1 Mile striders; 4 X 200m @ 80% w/ 200m jog recovery; 1 Mile jog <65%	4
Friday	3 Miles <70%	3
Saturday	4 Miles <70%	4
Sunday	OFF	0

Weekly Mileage	19
Hard Days	1

12 Week Program—Novice—Week 4

		Total Miles
Monday	3 Miles <70%	3
Tuesday	5 Miles <70%	5
Wednesday	OFF	0
Thursday	1 Mile jog <65%; 1 Mile striders; 3 X 400m @ 80% w/ 200m jog recovery; 1 Mile jog <65%	4
Friday	3 Miles <70%	3
Saturday	5 Miles <70%	5
Sunday	OFF	0
	Weekly/Monthly Mileage	20/75
	Hard Days	1

12 Week Program—Novice—Week 5

Novice Level:

WEEK 5

		Total Miles
Monday	5 Miles <70%	5
Tuesday	5 Miles <70%	5
Wednesday	OFF	0
Thursday	1 Mile jog <65%; 2 Miles @ 80%; 1 Mile jog <65%	4
Friday	3 Miles <70%	3
Saturday	5 Miles <70%	5
Sunday	Off	0

Weekly Mileage 22
Hard Days 1

12 Week Program—Novice—Week 6

Novice Level:

WEEK 6

		Total Miles
Monday	5 Miles <70%	5
Tuesday	5 Miles <70%	5
Wednesday	OFF	0
Thursday	1 Mile jog <65%; 1 Mile striders; 4 X 200m @ 80-85% w/ 200m jog recovery; 1 Mile jog <65%	4
Friday	3 Miles <70%	3
Saturday	5 Miles <70%	5
Sunday	OFF	0

Weekly Mileage 22
Hard Days 1

12 Week Program—Novice—Week 7

Novice Level:

WEEK 7

		Total Miles
Monday	5 Miles <70%	5
Tuesday	5 Miles <70%	5
Wednesday	3 Miles <70%	3
Thursday	1 Mile jog <65%; 1 Mile striders; 4 X 400m @ 80-85% w/ 200m jog recovery; 1 Mile jog <65%	5
Friday	3 Miles <70%	3
Saturday	5 Miles <70%	5
Sunday	OFF	0

Weekly Mileage	26
Hard Days	1

12 Week Program—Novice—Week 8

Novice Level:

WEEK 8

		Total Miles
Monday	5 Miles <70%	5
Tuesday	5 Miles <70%	5
Wednesday	3 Miles <70%	3
Thursday	1 Mile jog <65%; 3 Miles @ 80%; 1 Mile jog <65%	4
Friday	3 Miles <70%	3
Saturday	5 Miles <70%	5
Sunday	Off	0

Weekly/Monthly Mileage   25/95

Hard Days   1

12 Week Program—Novice—Week 9

		Total Miles
Monday	5 Miles <70%	5
Tuesday	5 Miles <70%	5
Wednesday	3 Miles <70%	3
Thursday	1 Mile jog <65%; 1 Mile striders; 6 X 200m @ 85% w/ 200m jog recovery; 1 Mile jog <65%	4
Friday	3 Miles <70%	3
Saturday	5 Miles <70%	5
Sunday	Off	0

Weekly Mileage	25
Hard Days	1

12 Week Program—Novice—Week 10

		Total Miles
Monday	5 Miles <70%	5
Tuesday	5 Miles <70%	5
Wednesday	5 Miles <70%	5
Thursday	1 Mile jog <65%; 1 Mile striders; 4 X 400m @ 85% w/ 200m jog recovery; 1 Mile jog <65%	5
Friday	3 Miles <70%	3
Saturday	6 Miles <70%	6
Sunday	Off	0

Weekly Mileage 29
Hard Days 1

12 Week Program—Novice—Week 11

		Total Miles
Monday	5 Miles <70%	5
Tuesday	1 Mile jog <65%; 3 Miles @ 80-85%; 1 Mile jog <65%	5
Wednesday	3 Miles <70%	5
Thursday	5 Miles <70%	5
Friday	1 Mile jog <65%; 1 Mile striders; 6 X 200m @ 85-90% w/ 200m jog recovery; 1 Mile jog <65%	4
Saturday	5 Miles <70%	5
Sunday	Off	0

Weekly Mileage	29
Hard Days	2

12 Week Program—Novice—Week 12

Novice Level:

WEEK 12

Total Miles

Monday	1 Mile jog <65%; 1 Mile striders; 1 Mile @95%; 1 Mile jog <65%	4
Tuesday	3 Miles <70%	3
Wednesday	1 Mile jog <65%; 1 Mile striders; 3 X 200m @ 95% w/ 110 jog recovery; 1 Mile jog <65%	4
Thursday	3 Miles <70%	3
Friday	1 Mile jog <65%; 1 Mile striders	
Saturday	RACE	6
Sunday	Off	0
	Weekly/Monthly Mileage	20/103
	Hard Days	3

12 Week Program—Intermediate— Week 1

Intermediate:

WEEK 1

		Total Miles
Monday	1 Mile jog <65%; 1 Mile @ 80%; 1 Mile jog <65%	3
Tuesday	3 Miles <70%	3
Wednesday	3 Miles <70%	3
Thursday	1 Mile jog <65%; 1/2 Mile striders; 4 X 400m @ 85% w/ 200m jog recovery; 1 Mile jog <65%	4
Friday	3 Miles <70%	3
Saturday	3 Miles <70%	3
Sunday	Off	0

Weekly Mileage	19
Hard Days	2

12 Week Program—Intermediate—Week 2

Intermediate:

WEEK 2

Total Miles

Monday	1 Mile jog <65%; 1 Mile @ 80%; 1 Mile jog <65%	3
Tuesday	3 Miles <70%	3
Wednesday	4 Miles <70%	4
Thursday	1 Mile jog <65%; 1 Mile striders; 3 X 800m @ 85% w/ 200m jog recovery; 1 Mile jog <65%	5
Friday	3 Miles <70%	3
Saturday	4 Miles <70%	4
Sunday	Off	0

Weekly Mileage 22
Hard Days 2

142

12 Week Program—Intermediate—Week 3

Intermediate:

WEEK 3

		Total Miles
Monday	2 Mile jog <65%; 2 Miles @ 80%; 1 Mile jog <65%	5
Tuesday	3 Miles <70%	3
Wednesday	4 Miles <70%	4
Thursday	1 Mile jog <65%; 1 Mile striders; 6 X 400m @ 85% w/ 200m jog recovery; 1 Mile jog <65%	5
Friday	3 Miles <70%	3
Saturday	4 Miles <70%	4
Sunday	Off	0

Weekly Mileage	24
Hard Days	2

12 Week Program—Intermediate—Week 4

Total Miles

Monday	1 Mile jog <65%; 3 Miles @ 80%; 1 Mile jog <65%	5
Tuesday	4 Miles <70%	4
Wednesday	5 Miles <70%	5
Thursday	1 Mile jog <65%; 1 Mile striders; 4 X 800m @ 85% w/ 200m jog recovery; 1 Mile jog <65%	6
Friday	4 Miles <70%	4
Saturday	5 Miles <70%	5
Sunday	Off	0

Weekly/Monthly Mileage   29/94

Hard Days   2

144

12 Week Program—Intermediate— Week 5

Intermediate:

WEEK 5

Total Miles

Monday	1 Mile jog <65%; 3 Miles @ 80%; 1 Mile jog <65%	5
Tuesday	5 Miles <70%	5
Wednesday	5 Miles <70%	5
Thursday	1 Mile jog <65%; 1 Mile striders; 6 X 400m @ 85% w/ 200m jog recovery; 1 Mile jog <65%	5
Friday	5 Miles <70%	5
Saturday	5 Miles <70%	5
Sunday	Off	0

Weekly Mileage 30
Hard Days 2

12 Week Program—Intermediate— Week 6

Intermediate:

WEEK 6

		Total Miles
Monday	1 Mile jog <65%; 4 Miles @ 80%; 1 Mile jog <65%	6
Tuesday	5 Miles <70%	5
Wednesday	6 Miles <70%	6
Thursday	1 Mile jog <65%; 1 Mile striders; 4 X 800m @ 85% w/ 200m jog recovery; 1 Mile jog <65%	6
Friday	5 Miles <70%	5
Saturday	6 Miles <70%	6
Sunday	Off	0

Weekly Mileage	34
Hard Days	2

146

12 Week Program—Intermediate— Week 7

WEEK 7

		Total Miles
Monday	1 Mile jog <65%; 4 Miles @ 80%; 1 Mile jog <65%	6
Tuesday	6 Miles <70%	6
Wednesday	6 Miles <70%	6
Thursday	1 Mile jog <65%; 1 Mile striders; 6 X 400m @ 85-90% w/ 200m jog recovery; 1 Mile jog <65%	5
Friday	6 Miles <70%	6
Saturday	6 Miles <70%	6
Sunday	Off	0

Weekly Mileage	35
Hard Days	2

12 Week Program—Intermediate— Week 8

Intermediate:

WEEK 8

Total Miles

Monday	1 Mile jog <65%; 1 Mile striders; 3 Miles @ 80-85%; 1 Mile jog <65%	6
Tuesday	6 Miles <70%	6
Wednesday	8 Miles <70%	8
Thursday	1 Mile jog <65%; 1 Mile striders; 4 X 800m @ 85-90% w/ 200m jog recovery; 1 Mile jog <65%	6
Friday	6 Miles <70%	6
Saturday	8 Miles <70%	8
Sunday	Off	0
	Weekly/Monthly Mileage	40/139
	Hard Days	2

12 Week Program—Intermediate— Week 9

Intermediate:

WEEK 9

		Total Miles
Monday	1 Mile jog <65%; 1 Mile striders; 3 Miles @ 85%; 1 Mile jog <65%	6
Tuesday	6 Miles <70%	6
Wednesday	8 Miles <70%	8
Thursday	1 Mile jog <65%; 1 Mile striders; 6 X 400m @ 85-90% w/ 200m jog recovery; 1 Mile jog <65%	5
Friday	6 Miles <70%	6
Saturday	8 Miles <70%	8
Sunday	Off	0
	Weekly Mileage	39
	Hard Days	2

12 Week Program—Intermediate—Week 10

Intermediate:

WEEK 10

		Total Miles
Monday	1 Mile jog <65%; 1 Mile striders; 3 Miles @ 85%; 1 Mile jog <65%	6
Tuesday	6 Miles <70%	6
Wednesday	8 Miles <70%	8
Thursday	1 Mile jog <65%; 1 Mile striders; 4 X 800m @ 90-95% w/ 200m jog recovery; 1 Mile jog <65%	6
Friday	6 Miles <70%	6
Saturday	8 Miles <70%	8
Sunday	Off	0
	Weekly Mileage	40
	Hard Days	2

12 Week Program—Intermediate— Week 11

Intermediate:

WEEK 11

		Total Miles
Monday	2 Mile jog <65%; 1 Mile striders; 2 Miles @90%; 3 Miles jog <65%	8
Tuesday	6 Miles <70%	6
Wednesday	8 Miles <70%	8
Thursday	2 Mile jog <65%; 2 Miles striders; 3 X 800m @ 95-100% w/ 200m jog recovery; 1 Mile jog <65%	7
Friday	6 Miles <70%	6
Saturday	8 Miles <70%	8
Sunday	Off	0
	Weekly Mileage	43
	Hard Days	2

12 Week Program—Intermediate— Week 12

Intermediate:

WEEK 12

Total Miles

Monday	2 Mile jog <65%; 1 Mile striders; 1 Mile @ 95%; 2 Mile jog <65%	6
Tuesday	4 Miles <70%	6
Wednesday	2 Mile jog <65%; 1 Mile striders; 4 X 200m @ 95-100% w/ 110 jog recovery; 1 Mile jog <65%	5
Thursday	4 Miles <70%	6
Friday	1 Mile jog <65%; 1 Mile striders; 1 Mile jog <65%	3
Saturday	RACE	6
Sunday	Off	0

Weekly/Monthly Mileage 32/154
Hard Days 3

12 Week Program—Advanced—Week 1

Advanced:

WEEK 1

		Total Miles
Monday	4 Miles <70%	4
Tuesday	2 Mile jog <65%; 2 Miles @ 80%; 2 Mile jog <65%	6
Wednesday	4 Miles <70%	4
Thursday	5 Miles <70%	5
Friday	1 Mile jog <65%; 1 Mile striders; 6 x 400m @ 85% w/ 200m jog recovery; 1 Mile jog <65%	5
Saturday	3 Miles <70%	3
Sunday	6 Miles @ 70-75%	6

Weekly Mileage	33
Hard Days	3

12 Week Program—Advanced—Week 2

Advanced:

WEEK 2

		Total Miles
Monday	4 Miles <70%	4
Tuesday	2 Mile jog <65%; 2 Miles @ 80%; 2 Mile jog <65%	6
Wednesday	4 Miles <70%	4
Thursday	5 Miles <70%	5
Friday	1 Mile jog <65%; 1 Mile striders; 4 X 800m @ 85% w/ 200m jog recovery; 1 Mile jog <65%	6
Saturday	3 Miles <70%	3
Sunday	8 Miles @ 70-75%	8

Weekly Mileage	36
Hard Days	3

154

12 Week Program—Advanced—Week 3

Advanced:

WEEK 3

		Total Miles
Monday	5 Miles <70%	5
Tuesday	2 Mile jog <65%; 3 Miles @ 80%; 2 Mile jog <65%	7
Wednesday	5 Miles <70%	5
Thursday	5 Miles <70%	5
Friday	1 Mile jog <65%; 1 Mile striders; 8 x 400m @ 85% w/ 200m jog recovery; 1 Mile jog <65%	6
Saturday	4 Miles <70%	4
Sunday	8 Miles @ 70-75%	8

Weekly Mileage	40
Hard Days	3

12 Week Program—Advanced—Week 4

Advanced:

WEEK 4

		Total Miles
Monday	5 Miles <70%	5
Tuesday	2 Mile jog <65%; 3 Miles @ 80%; 2 Mile jog <65%	7
Wednesday	5 Miles <70%	5
Thursday	5 Miles <70%	5
Friday	1 Mile jog <65%; 1 Mile striders; 5 X 800m @ 85% w/ 200m jog recovery; 1 Mile jog <65%	6
Saturday	4 Miles <70%	4
Sunday	10 Miles @ 70-75%	10

Weekly/Monthly Mileage	42/151
Hard Days	3

12 Week Program—Advanced—Week 5

Advanced:

WEEK 5

		Total Miles
Monday	5 Miles <70%	5
Tuesday	2 Mile jog <65%; 3 Miles @ 80%; 2 Mile jog <65%	7
Wednesday	5 Miles <70%	5
Thursday	6 Miles <70%	6
Friday	1 Mile jog <65%; 1 Mile striders; 8 x 400m @ 85% w/ 200m jog recovery; 1 Mile jog <65%	6
Saturday	4 Miles <70%	4
Sunday	10 Miles @ 70-75%	10

Weekly Mileage 43
Hard Days 3

12 Week Program—Advanced—Week 6

Advanced:

WEEK 6

		Total Miles
Monday	5 Miles <70%	5
Tuesday	2 Mile jog <65%; 4 Miles @ 80%; 2 Mile jog <65%	8
Wednesday	5 Miles <70%	5
Thursday	6 Miles <70%	6
Friday	1 Mile jog <65%; 1 Mile striders; 5 X 800m @ 85-90% w/ 200m jog recovery; 1 Mile jog <65%	6
Saturday	4 Miles <70%	4
Sunday	10 Miles @ 70-75%	10

Weekly Mileage	44
Hard Days	3

12 Week Program—Advanced—Week 7

Advanced:

WEEK 7

		Total Miles
Monday	6 Miles <70%	6
Tuesday	2 Mile jog <65%; 4 Miles @ 80%; 2 Mile jog <65%	8
Wednesday	6 Miles <70%	6
Thursday	6 Miles <70%	6
Friday	1 Mile jog <65%; 1 Mile striders; 8 x 400m @ 85-90% w/ 200m jog recovery; 1 Mile jog <65%	6
Saturday	6 Miles <70%	6
Sunday	10 Miles @ 70-75%	10
	Weekly Mileage	48
	Hard Days	3

12 Week Program—Advanced—Week 8

Advanced:

WEEK 8

		Total Miles
Monday	6 Miles <70%	6
Tuesday	1 Mile jog <65%; 1 Mile striders; 4 Miles @ 80-85%; 2 Mile jog <65%	8
Wednesday	6 Miles <70%	6
Thursday	8 Miles <70%	8
Friday	1 Mile jog <65%; 1 Mile striders; 6 X 800m @ 85-90% w/ 200m jog recovery; 1 Mile jog <65%	7
Saturday	6 Miles <70%	6
Sunday	10 Miles @ 70-75%	10
	Weekly/Monthly Mileage	51/186
	Hard Days	3

12 Week Program—Advanced—Week 9

Advanced:

WEEK 9

		Total Miles
Monday	8 Miles <70%	8
Tuesday	1 Mile jog <65%; 1 Mile striders; 4 Miles @ 85%; 2 Mile jog <65%	8
Wednesday	6 Miles <70%	6
Thursday	8 Miles <70%	8
Friday	1 Mile jog <65%; 1 Mile striders; 8 x 400m @ 90-95% w/ 200m jog recovery; 1 Mile jog <65%	6
Saturday	6 Miles <70%	6
Sunday	12 Miles @ 70-75%	12
	Weekly Mileage	54
	Hard Days	3

12 Week Program—Advanced—Week 10

		Total Miles
Monday	8 Miles <70%	8
Tuesday	1 Mile jog <65%; 1 Mile striders; 4 Miles @ 85%; 2 Mile jog <65%	8
Wednesday	6 Miles <70%	6
Thursday	8 Miles <70%	8
Friday	1 Mile jog <65%; 1 Mile striders; 6 X 800m @ 90-95% w/ 200m jog recovery; 1 Mile jog <65%	7
Saturday	6 Miles <70%	6
Sunday	12 Miles @ 70-75%	12
	Weekly Mileage	55
	Hard Days	3

12 Week Program—Advanced—Week 11

Advanced:

WEEK 11

		Total Miles
Monday	8 Miles <70%	8
Tuesday	1 Mile jog <65%; 1 Mile striders; 3 Miles @ 90%; 2 Mile jog <65%	7
Wednesday	6 Miles <70%	6
Thursday	6 Miles <70%	6
Friday	1 Mile jog <65%; 1 Mile striders; 4 X 800m @ 95-100% w/ 200m jog recovery; 1 Mile jog <65%	6
Saturday	6 Miles <70%	6
Sunday	6 Miles <70%	6
	Weekly Mileage	45
	Hard Days	2

12 Week Program—Advanced—Week 12

Advanced:

WEEK 12

		Total Miles
Monday	6 Miles <70%	6
Tuesday	1 Mile jog <65%; 1 Mile striders; 2 Miles @ 95%; 2 Mile jog <65%	6
Wednesday	4 Miles <70%	4
Thursday	1 Mile jog <65%; 1 Mile striders; 4 X 200m @ 95-100% w/ 110 jog recovery; 1 Mile jog <65%	4
Friday	1 Mile jog <65%; 1 Mile striders; 1 Mile jog <65%	3
Saturday	RACE	6
Sunday	6 Miles <70%	6
	Weekly/Monthly Mileage	35/189
	Hard Days	3

12 Week Program—Competitive— Week 1

Competitive:

WEEK 1

		Total Miles
Monday	6 Miles <70%	6
Tuesday	2 Mile jog <65%; 3 Miles @ 80%; 2 Mile jog <65%	7
Wednesday	6 Miles <70%	6
Thursday	7 Miles <70%	7
Friday	2 Mile jog <65%; 1 Mile striders; 6 x 400m @ 85% w/ 200m jog recovery; 2 Mile jog <65%	7
Saturday	4 Miles <70%	4
Sunday	8 Miles @ 70-75%	8
	Weekly Mileage	45
	Hard Days	3

12 Week Program—Competitive— Week 2

Competitive:

WEEK 2

Total Miles

Monday	6 Miles <70%	6
Tuesday	2 Mile jog <65%; 3 Miles @ 80%; 2 Mile jog <65%	7
Wednesday	6 Miles <70%	6
Thursday	7 Miles <70%	7
Friday	2 Mile jog <65%; 1 Mile striders; 4 X 800m @ 85% w/ 200m jog recovery; 2 Mile jog <65%	8
Saturday	4 Miles <70%	4
Sunday	10 Miles @ 70-75%	10

Weekly Mileage 48
Hard Days 3

12 Week Program—Competitive—Week 3

Competitive:

WEEK 3

		Total Miles
Monday	7 Miles <70%	7
Tuesday	2 Mile jog <65%; 4 Miles @ 80%; 2 Mile jog <65%	8
Wednesday	7 Miles <70%	7
Thursday	7 Miles <70%	7
Friday	2 Mile jog <65%; 1 Mile striders; 8 x 400m @ 85% w/ 200m jog recovery; 2 Mile jog <65%	8
Saturday	6 Miles <70%	6
Sunday	10 Miles @ 70-75%	10

Weekly Mileage	53
Hard Days	3

12 Week Program—Competitive—Week 4

		Total Miles
Monday	7 Miles <70%	7
Tuesday	2 Mile jog <65%; 4 Miles @ 80%; 2 Mile jog <65%	8
Wednesday	7 Miles <70%	7
Thursday	7 Miles <70%	7
Friday	1 Mile jog <65%; 1 Mile striders; 6 X 800m @ 85% w/ 200m jog recovery; 1 Mile jog <65%	7
Saturday	6 Miles <70%	6
Sunday	12 Miles @ 70-75%	12

Weekly/Monthly Mileage	54/200
Hard Days	3

168

12 Week Program—Competitive—Week 5

Competitive:

WEEK 5

		Total Miles
Monday	7 Miles <70%	7
Tuesday	2 Mile jog <65%; 4 Miles @ 80%; 2 Mile jog <65%	8
Wednesday	7 Miles <70%	7
Thursday	10 Miles <70%	10
Friday	1 Mile jog <65%; 1 Mile striders; 10 x 400m @ 85% w/ 200m jog recovery; 1 Mile jog <65%	7
Saturday	6 Miles <70%	6
Sunday	12 Miles @ 70-75%	12
	Weekly Mileage	57
	Hard Days	3

12 Week Program—Competitive— Week 6

Competitive:

WEEK 6

		Total Miles
Monday	7 Miles <70%	7
Tuesday	2 Mile jog <65%; 5 Miles @ 80%; 2 Mile jog <65%	9
Wednesday	7 Miles <70%	7
Thursday	10 Miles <70%	10
Friday	1 Mile jog <65%; 1 Mile striders; 6 X 800m @ 85-90% w/ 200m jog recovery; 1 Mile jog <65%	7
Saturday	6 Miles <70%	6
Sunday	12 Miles @ 70-75%	12
	Weekly Mileage	58
	Hard Days	3

12 Week Program—Competitive— Week 7

Competitive:

WEEK 7

		Total Miles
Monday	8 Miles <70%	8
Tuesday	2 Mile jog <65%; 5 Miles @ 80%; 2 Mile jog < 65%	9
Wednesday	8 Miles <70%	8
Thursday	10 Miles <70%	10
Friday	1 Mile jog <65%; 1 Mile striders; 10 x 400m @ 85-90% w/ 200m jog recovery; 1 Mile jog < 65%	7
Saturday	6 Miles <70%	6
Sunday	12 Miles @ 70-75%	12

Weekly Mileage 60
Hard Days 3

12 Week Program—Competitive—Week 8

Total Miles

Monday	8 Miles <70%	8
Tuesday	1 Mile jog <65%; 1 Mile striders; 5 Miles @ 80-85%; 2 Mile jog <65%	9
Wednesday	8 Miles <70%	8
Thursday	10 Miles <70%	10
Friday	1 Mile jog <65%; 1 Mile striders; 6 X 800m @ 85-90% w/ 200m jog recovery; 1 Mile jog <65%	7
Saturday	6 Miles <70%	6
Sunday	12 Miles @ 70-75%	12
	Weekly/Monthly Mileage	60/235
	Hard Days	3

12 Week Program—Competitive— Week 9

Competitive:

WEEK 9

		Total Miles
Monday	8 Miles <70%	8
Tuesday	1 Mile jog <65%; 1 Mile striders; 5 Miles @ 85%; 2 Mile jog <65%	9
Wednesday	8 Miles <70%	8
Thursday	10 Miles <70%	10
Friday	1 Mile jog <65%; 1 Mile striders; 10 x 400m @ 90-95% w/ 200m jog recovery; 1 Mile jog <65%	7
Saturday	6 Miles <70%	6
Sunday	14 Miles @ 70-75%	14
	Weekly Mileage	62
	Hard Days	3

12 Week Program—Competitive— Week 10

Competitive:

WEEK 10

Total Miles

Monday	8 Miles <70%	8
Tuesday	1 Mile jog <65%; 1 Mile striders; 5 Miles @ 85%; 2 Mile jog <65%	9
Wednesday	6 Miles <70%	6
Thursday	8 Miles <70%	8
Friday	1 Mile jog <65%; 1 Mile striders; 6 X 800m @ 90-95% w/ 200m jog recovery; 1 Mile jog <65%	7
Saturday	6 Miles <70%	6
Sunday	14 Miles @ 70-75%	14

Weekly Mileage 58

Hard Days 3

12 Week Program—Competitive—
Week 11

Competitive:

WEEK 11

		Total Miles
Monday	8 Miles <70%	8
Tuesday	1 Mile jog <65%; 1 Mile striders; 5 Miles @ 90%; 2 Mile jog <65%	9
Wednesday	6 Miles <70%	6
Thursday	8 Miles <70%	8
Friday	1 Mile jog <65%; 1 Mile striders; 4 X 800m @ 95-100% w/ 200m jog recovery; 1 Mile jog <65%	6
Saturday	6 Miles <70%	6
Sunday	6 Miles <70%	6
	Weekly Mileage	49
	Hard Days	2

12 Week Program—Competitive— Week 12

Competitive:

WEEK 12

Total Miles

Monday	6 Miles <70%	6
Tuesday	1 Mile jog <65%;1 Mile striders; 3 Miles @ 95%; 2 Mile jog <65%	7
Wednesday	6 Miles <70%	6
Thursday	1 Mile jog <65%; 1 Mile striders; 4 X 200m @ 95-100% w/ 110 jog recovery; 1 Mile jog <65%	4
Friday	1 Mile jog <65%; 1 Mile striders; 1 Mile jog <65%	3
Saturday	RACE	6
Sunday	6 Miles <70%	6

Weekly/Monthly Mileage 38/207
Hard Days 2

15. Secrets and Tips

There are a lot of little truisms, secrets, and bits of information heart monitor users accumulate after awhile. They don't seem to fit anywhere else, so I've gathered them together in this chapter to help you flatten out your learning curve.

Sticking Points

When I first started using a monitor, I discovered that I seemed to have a pace that felt "grooved in." It was several beats above my 70% recovery ceiling, so it was annoying to have to back off from this very natural-feeling pace. Other monitor users reported the same thing. I started calling this particular heart rate a "sticking point."

The main thing is, don't give in to it. If you allow yourself to go over your ceiling regularly, it will just slow down your progress. I discovered after I began to get into shape that the sticking point seemed to go away.

Your Cheatin' Heart:
Hills, Comebacks, etc.

When it's okay to "cheat" on your monitor

Okay, I admit that I fudge on the heart monitor a little. Sometimes a lot. Here are some typical situations:

Hills: It's flat as a proverbial pancake where I run in north Florida, but there are a few slight bumps in the landscape. If the monitor chirps on me a few times on these elevations, I don't worry about it. You shouldn't either. The problem comes when you start disregarding the monitor altogether. You get tired of hearing the beep and turn it off, or you set it higher, or you just tune it out. Basically, you're back to training-as-usual. You may be *wearing* a heart monitor, but that doesn't mean you're doing heart monitor training.

Coming back: When I'm coming back from a layoff, for illness, injury, travel, whatever, I find my heart rate soaring on the first few runs. I don't worry about staying completely under 70% during those first days back. After all, the general strategy of recovery days is to preserve glycogen, and when you've had a layoff, you're chock full of glycogen. You can get stricter on yourself after three or four days.

Bad Days: We all have them. Sometimes they mean that you're fighting off a bug, sometimes that you're overtrained. So maybe you have to cheat a little to get through this run. Okay, but be aware of what's going on.

Heat can be a killer

Heat: Yes, I admit that I occasionally cheat a little on hot days. See more on this below.

Lost Days: Some days you'll go out for a 70% recovery run and it just wasn't meant to happen. You get happy feet, you find yourself running with an overly enthusiastic partner, whatever. Your monitor starts beeping early and keeps beeping. Sometimes it's best just to punt. On those occasions I'll simply go with the flow, count that day as a tempo run, and then rearrange my schedule so that one or two recovery days follow.

Heat

Runners often ask about how heat affects heart rate. Living and training mostly in Florida, I consider myself a front porch Ph.D in this subject. And I can say with some confidence: Training in hot weather will cause your heart rate to soar, as your system sends a lot of your blood supply to the surface of your skin in an attempt to cool your body. This is particularly true after the first 30 minutes or so of running, when your core temperature has risen dramatically. What this means is simply that you have to slow down—sometimes drastically—in hot weather to stay under your ceiling.

After the first 30 minutes, heat is a big factor

A similar phenomenon takes place at altitude, and I have heard cold weather may have such an effect, but I've seen no documentation on it.

The Lag Rule: Keep Watching

Your heart rate will lag behind your your body. You'll hit a hill, and it will take several seconds before you see the rate going up. It's more pronounced the other way. You'll hear the alarm go off, start slowing down, and it will seem like it takes forever to get your heart rate under control. Some of this is caused by the design of the monitor, which is programmed in such a way as to ignore potentially erroneous signals until a rate is substantiated.

But some of the lag is physiological. When your body goes into oxygen debt, your heart works for a few seconds even harder after you begin resting. That's why you need to keep watching it after an interval or at the end of a race, to see the very highest rate it will get to.

But here is another truism: the better shape you get into, the quicker your heart rate responds to both effort and rest. See the next item.

Quick Monitor Response = Fitness

As you get into better shape, you'll notice the "lag time" gets shorter and shorter. Doing intervals, you'll see a high point a few seconds after a repeat, then the heart rate will plummet rapidly. As you start your daily run, the monitor will build quickly from your resting rate of 55 or 60 and go right to 120 or 130 in the first few minutes. This quick response, both up and down, is a good indicator of fitness.

Daily Real World Biofeedback

Measuring the stress in daily life

Some athletes have experimented with wearing their monitors around in the real world during the day, just to see what's going on with their bodies. Try it sometime. You'll find out just how much wear and tear that annoying boss or coworker is really causing you. Or the toll that the traffic in your city is really taking on you. Or how restful a moment's meditation in a quiet corner can really be.

The Urination Riddle

A request to urologists in the audience

This is a bizarre little observation, apropos of nothing in particular, but I have noticed that for some reason if you stop in the middle of a run to urinate, your heart rate goes up. Occasionally, you'll be running well under your 70% ceiling, stop to water the bushes, and suddenly your alarm will go off. (It goes back down very quickly, of course.)

I once mentioned this to the president of one of

the heart monitor manufacturers, and he was unaware of it. If there's a urologist out there who can fill me in, I'd love to hear an explanation of this phenomenon.

Artifacts: poor contact, power lines, etc.

The semi-realistic bogus readings are hard to spot

Athletes often get erroneous readings when they first start a workout. Usually, they are so far off the chart (like a reading of 220 in the first few steps of a run) you won't have any problem interpreting the reading as bogus. But I've noticed that you can also get a semi-realistic bogus reading early on, a reading only 20 or 30 beats off. For instance, occasionally I'll see a 160 or 165 when I know for dead certain I'm only at 120 or 130.

The problem is often poor contact

These early erroneous readings are almost all caused by poor contact of your skin to the chest strap receptors. Just find these areas on the underside of your chest strap (it's usually a groove-patterned area), and moisten them with saliva. I've gotten so I can manage this without taking the strap off, though I occasionally get strange looks from passersby.

Other bogus signals, as I've mentioned elsewhere, can come from transmission lines or towers, other runners' monitors, or car or motorcycle engines. Usually these signals are so out of whack you'll have no trouble interpreting them.

Sometimes a "crazy" heart rate is real

On the other hand, occasionally you'll see some surprising heart rates and there won't be any ready explanation. I've seen runners who apparently respond physiologically to the fact that they are watching their own heart rate (hi, Delores!). Perhaps it's an all-too-real reminder of their mortality, like looking at your own x-rays. In any event, they suddenly find their heart rate shooting up from a normal daytime rate of 60, 70, or 80 to way over 100.

Before a workout I often note my heart rate going up, apparently just in anticipation. No cause for alarm in these cases; they are all normal phenomena.

The Two-Mile Rule

I try to be Mr. Flexibility when it comes to hard workouts. If I'm scheduled for hard intervals or a tempo run, and I'm not feeling right, I don't have any qualms about substituting an easy recovery run and postponing the hard stuff until the next day. Sometimes I will put off harder stuff for several days in a row.

The Two-Mile Rule is especially important on hard days

But I don't try to decide these things before the run. I don't even decide after the first mile. I've mentioned the Two-Mile Rule before, but it's especially applicable to hard days: I always wait until at least two miles into the warm-up to decide how I really feel, sometimes longer. There's no scientific basis for it, just a very subjective observation based on years of experience that it's hard to get a reading on your own body until after you get it cranked up a bit.

Occasionally you'll have a good workout on a day when you feel pretty blah just walking around. Sometimes you'll get just the opposite result. And it seems to only get more difficult to judge these things as you get into better shape. Go figure. But do yourself a favor and don't make any rash workout plans based on how you feel planting your tootsies on the floor first thing in the morning.

The dangers of hanging with the group

Running With So-called Friends

This is one of the biggest problems athletes have when switching to a heart monitor program. You can bet that the group you're training with now is going too hard most of the time.

One possible solution is to run alone on recovery days (or even with a slower group), then run with your old crew on a day that's supposed to be a tempo run anyway.

The key is to break out of the old pattern, and you'll never do it by just strapping on a heart monitor and hopping in with the same old crowd. Not only will you take a lot of abuse for using "that new fangled gadget," but you'll blow your training program.

Different Strokes: Comfort Zones Vary

Milers and marathoners may have different comfort zones

Different athletes seem to perform with different comfort levels at the same nominal effort as gauged by the heart monitor. What am I saying in English? That my 80% may be harder for me to maintain than your 80%. Some of that may be simply a result of different fitness levels. After all, one component of fitness is the ability to maintain a given effort level for longer periods of time. But I suspect there may be more to it than that. Different athletes have different muscle type composition and different efficiencies at various paces. A true long distance runner with a heavy concentration of slow-twitch muscle fibers will probably be able to run very comfortably in the 75-80% of max ranges, but find it harder to get up over 85%, or the Aerobic Threshold ranges, where more and more reliance on anaerobic systems come into play. A miler, on the other hand, may find it quite comfortable to run at 85 to 90%, at least until he begins to build up sufficient lactic acid to slow him down.

The Interval Workout Reset

For reasons unknown to me, after my first several interval or tempo sessions in any given buildup, I often find my 70% recovery pace to be pleasantly swifter the next day. In other words, I'm running faster, yet still staying under my ceiling. (This also happens sometimes after a race.) It's as if the intense work has somehow reset my tachometer and suddenly I'm able to sustain a pace that would have been over 70% previously.

Coaches with Budget Problems

High school and college coaches can use heart monitors to great advantage, since young, eager athletes are among the worst offenders when it comes to violating the hard/easy principle.

Using monitors with teams

The problem is how to go about outfitting a squad of 27 hellions when your budget barely allows for gas money to the state meet?

It's simple, really. Once you have determined actual max heart rates for everyone in the group, simply designate a number of "Rudolphs."

If you only have three monitors, you'll divide the squad by ability into three packs, and you'll have three Rudolphs, each picked for being right in the middle of his or her pack in terms of ability. On recovery runs you simply instruct the runners that no one gets ahead of their Rudolph, at risk of some awful penalty.

Picking your "Rudolphs"

Of course, there's a likelihood that some runners will have to run at 65% or even 60% to stay behind their Rudolph. Is that a problem? Not in the least. Those runners are still getting all the benefits of aerobic training and they're preserving even more glycogen than the 70% runners. They may grouse a little, but they'll be fine.

Now if you only have one monitor for an entire group of runners, you'll probably have way too much variation in ability to assign a single Rudolph. The slower ones will find the pace too fast and the blasters will be chomping at the bit. No one will be happy.

In such cases you might be better off using something like the "two-minute rule" to approximate the appropriate 70% pace for each group.

You know you're a runner when you . . .

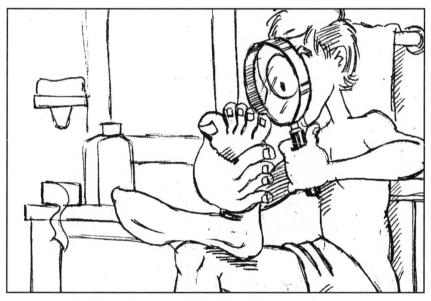

. . . spend a lot of time with your feet.

16. Using a Heart Monitor for Sports Other than Running

Nothing about heart rate monitor training is more confusing than trying to use them in secondary or multiple sports training. It makes a great deal of difference whether we are talking about a single-sport non-running athlete, a single-sport athlete switching to another single sport, a single sport athlete using another sport for cross-training purposes, or a multi-sport athlete simply looking to use the heart monitor to maximize training efficiencies in each individual discipline. Because of the potential for creating even more misunderstanding, let's take each situation separately.

Non-running Single-sport Athletes

This is the easy one. All of the physiological principles discussed earlier that apply to runners apply equally to other disciplines. The muscle groups affected are different, of course, but the problems and challenges parallel those of the runner.

An athlete switching from one endurance sport to another may at first find his or her heart rate ranges to be confusing. For instance, a runner

Switching sports can be confusing to monitor users

undertaking swim training will find it difficult to get his or her heart rate up to the same ranges easily achieved by running. This phenomenon seems to be related to the fact that the undertrained specific muscles required for the new sport simply are not sufficiently strong to support exertion that the cardiovascular system is otherwise capable of. In other words, a runner with an actual max of 200 may not be a good enough swimmer or biker to get anywhere close to that number in the water or on two wheels. As the athlete becomes more proficient at the new sport, this phenomenon disappears.

Other sports can be more forgiving than running

Another phenomenon that should be pointed out is that running is perhaps the single most traumatic endurance sport from a biomechanical perspective, and thus overtraining problems tend to show up earlier in runners than in other disciplines simply because the effects of gravity and shock are so much more pronounced in running than in non-weight-bearing sports such as swimming, cycling, rowing, and to a lesser extent the other weight-bearing but less traumatic sports such as cross-country skiing, speed skating, and so on. But that means that in other sports there is much more of a margin for error, much more leeway for training errors to be compounded before such inefficiencies take their toll in the realm of performance.

Put more simply: a runner on an overly ambitious training regimen may well begin paying the price in a few days; a swimmer or cyclist may struggle along for weeks or even months before coming to grips with the problem.

Is there too much intensity in non-weight-bearing sports?

For that reason, I believe that coaches in many of the non-running sports make the mistake of including too much intensity too often in their training regimens. A good example is swimming, in which many programs will have athletes doing intensity (in other words, intervals) twice a day, seven days a week!

Yet the basic challenge facing all single-sport endurance athletes is essentially the same as the one facing runners: building an aerobic base through long, less-intense effort, and sharpening that base with shorter, more intense anaerobic work. And, as is surely clear by now, to my way of thinking the most efficient way to do that is by preserving glycogen during easier, aerobic workouts, allowing the athlete to get the maximum benefit from the more intense anaerobic work.

I admit that this takes a fair amount of gall, to advocate what amounts to a departure from training wisdom in disciplines in which I can claim no true expertise. On the other hand, as an "experiment of one," I can say unequivocally that the same approach I describe for running has worked equally well for me in swimming and cycling.

Heart monitoring works well in the other sports

Several years ago, when training seriously for the triathlon, I went on crash programs, at different times, in swimming and cycling. Immersing myself in one sport at a time in order to learn technique and maximize training efficiency, I found that I improved much more rapidly by interspersing 70% recovery days with intense days, though I often needed only a single recovery day instead of two or three.

Recovery needs are more subtle

The need for recovery was much more subtle because of the non-weight-bearing nature of the sports, but the same physiological principles seemed to apply: the rewards of preserving glycogen and enhancing fat-burning capacity by sub-70% effort were obvious.

With that in mind, here is how I would go about applying hard/easy heart monitor principles to other single sports.

Swimming

Some monitors will work in the water

Yes, you can use many heart monitors in the water (the Polar Favor is a good bet) and it's a good thing. Swimmers are notorious for doing intervals in most workouts. Strangely enough, runners went through a phase like this in the 1950s and early 60s when the training ideas of the great Czech runner Emil Zatopek and the influential Hungarian coach Mihaly Igloi were dominant in the U.S.[1] Many was the high school or college coach in that era who would daily tack up a workout that would look something like this:

Warm-up
20 X 400m w/ 3 min. rest
shower

Or, for variety:
Warm-up
30 X 200m w/ 1 min. rest
shower

The interval-only approach to training

This would go on day after day until an entire team was reduced to invalids and head cases.

Indeed, virtually a whole generation of American runners was burned out on running altogether by this obsession with interval training. Little wonder David Martin and Peter Coe concluded: "Over the years, the pendulum seems to have swung between the extremes of speed emphasis and endurance emphasis. But there is often little logic to fashion, and such extremes lack a sensible rationale. As with arguments, once both sides have been presented, the best solution is often an incorporation of an appropriate mix of each."[2]

Thankfully, runners have broken free of the track and now even the most dedicated milers and half-milers do a good bit of their training on the roads or trails. By and large, however, swimmers are still confined the to the pool and the interval workout.[3]

Here is a particularly unimaginative, though not all that unusual weekly swim schedule (with likely percentages of max shown in parentheses), and how I would alter it using the heart monitor principles elucidated earlier:

George Goodfin, Typical Week BEFORE HM Training

Mon   200M warm-up; 10 X 100M on 1:30 (90-95% of max); 200 cooldown

Tue   200M warm-up; 20 X 50M on 40 (90-95% of max); 200 cooldown

Wed   200M warm-up; 5 X 200M on 3:15 (90-95% of max); 200 cooldown

Thu   200M warm-up; 10 X 100M on 1:30 90-95% of max); 200 cooldown

Fri   200M warm-up; 20 X 50M on 40 (90-95% of max); 200 cooldown

Sat   200M warm-up; 5 X 200M on 3:15 (90-95% of max); 200 cooldown

Sun   200M warm-up; 1000M time trial (95-100%); 200M cooldown

Total yardage: 9800 meters
Total number of "hard" days: 7

George Goodfin, Typical Week
AFTER HM Training

Mon   500M mixed stroke warm-up <70%
             1000M continuous <70%; 200 cooldown

Tue   500M mixed stroke warm-up < 70%;
             15 X 100M on 1:45 (85%
             of max); 200 cooldown

Wed   500M mixed stroke warm-up <70%;
             1000M continuous <70%; 200 cooldown

Thu   500M mixed stroke warm-up <70%;
             1500M continuous <70%; 200 cooldown

Fri   500M mixed stroke warm-up < 70%;
             10 X 100M on 1:30 (90%
             of max); 200 cooldown

Sat   500M mixed stroke warm-up <70%;
             1000M continuous <70%; 200 cooldown

Sun   500M mixed stroke warm-up <70%;
             1000M time trial (95-100%);
             200M cooldown

Total yardage: 12,900 meters
Total number of "hard" days: 3

Admittedly, this is a simplistic example; most swimming programs are more varied than the "before" week shown here, both in stroke type and in interval distances. My point is that much, if not all, non-warm-up effort is in the 80-95% range. Such programs present the athlete with a daily grind that is deadening both physically and mentally. On competitive school teams that train twice daily, it's a wonder athletes last out the season.

By adding recovery days and easy yardage to the program, we can increase the overall distance covered, as well as improve the quality and quantity of the intense days. All by giving up the daily grind and by using the heart monitor to insure good recovery.

Cycling

Cyclists are as much prone to the daily 80-95% grind as any athletes.[4] Many train on hills, which means anaerobic effort, which means any thoughts of "spinning an easy 20" usually fly out the window at the first incline.

In non-weight-bearing sports the monitor still doesn't lie

As with swimming, the non-weight-bearing nature of the sport allows the athlete to return day after day for more of the same, with breakdowns and burnouts less frequent than those experienced by overtraining runners.

But once again, the monitor doesn't lie, and in my own "experiment of one" as a cyclist, I found the benefits of heart monitored hard/easy training to be striking. Keep in mind that we are still talking about single sport training here (though in my experiment the eventual goal was the triathlon). When mixing sports, as discussed later, the picture becomes more complex.

Here is a typical cyclist Before and After scenario.

Francis Fastpedal, Typical Training Week
BEFORE HM Training

Mon   25 miles @ 80-90% of max
Tue   25 miles @ 80-90% of max
Wed   25 miles @ 80-90% of max
Thu   25 miles @ 80-90% of max
Fri   25 miles @ 80-90% of max
Sat   50 miles @ 80-90% of max
Sun   25 miles @ 80-90% of max
Total mileage: 200
Total number of "hard" days: 7

Francis Fastpedal, Typical Training Week
AFTER HM Training

Mon   30 miles <70%
Tue   5 mile warm-up
       20 miles @ 80-85% of max
Wed   30 miles <70%
Thu   5 mile warm-up
       10 miles @ 80-85% of max
       10 miles hill jams @ 90-95% of max
Fri   30 miles <70%
Sat   30 miles <70%
Sun   75 miles @ 70-75%
Total mileage: 245
Total number of "hard" days: 3

I don't know if other runners have the same experience I do on the bike, but when I get to a hill, I find it very difficult to stay under 70% on the ascent. Maybe it's related to the pronounced impact grade has on speed, but something in me wants to attack the hill and keep attacking until it's crested. I don't have nearly the same problem on the flat. In any case, as in running, the temptation to break the

70% ceiling should be resisted as much as possible.

Cross-training

Athletes use the phrase "cross-training" to mean a lot of different things. To me, it has a very specific definition: the use of an alternative sport or activity to enhance performance in an athlete's primary sport.

Why cross train?

Thus cross-training may mean a runner lifting weights; it may mean a downhill skier doing roller blading, it may mean a cyclist doing some running.

The purpose is generally to provide an alternative training technique in order to work on a specific weakness, to avoid overuse injuries in the primary sport, or to avoid "staleness" or overtraining. Sometimes, as in the case of the roller-blading skier, the alternative sport is practiced in the off-season because the primary sport may not be available at all.

Muscle specificity is crucial to performance

Generally speaking, cross-training should be approached very carefully. Because of the principle of "muscle specificity," physiologists tell us that muscle cells trained by swimming will be of little or no use to us while running, and vice versa.[5]

And while there may certainly be some crossover benefits in some sports—cycling and running, for instance—there is no question that to get to be a good runner you must run; to be a good swimmer you must swim, and so on.

The trade off

This is not to deny the potential benefits of cross-training, particularly in overall health, strength, and flexibility. The question the athlete must answer is whether the amount of time spent on cross-training might be profitably spent on the primary sport and, if so, is the athlete prepared to give up enhanced performance in order to accomplish other more general health goals?

I have found that the most important benefits

of cross-training are the same ones available by practicing a heart monitor-enforced hard/easy training cycle as described in this book: recovery, injury prevention, and overall cardiovascular training.

I'm not alone in this view. Despite a certain trendiness in the late 1980s, cross-training appears to have lost favor among many experts. Coe and Martin, in *Training Distance Runners*, don't mention it, and Noakes, in *Lore of Running*, devotes less than a lukewarm page to the subject.[6]

Cross-training day = easy day

Nonetheless, if an athlete has made the decision to incorporate cross-training, it is a simple matter indeed to blend it in with a heart monitored hard/easy program. A cross-training day by definition uses little or no glycogen in the primary sport muscle cells and thus—like a day off—is simply counted as a recovery day.

Multi-Sport Competitions

Formula for disaster

Duathlon, triathlon, and other multi-sport events present the athlete with a difficult logistical proposition. Although many professional and some top amateur triathletes train in all three sports nearly every day,[7] for most mortals this is a formula for disaster, even if every attempt is made to apply and enforce the hard/easy principle. Since it would be a nightmare to attempt to do three hard workouts in a single day, the logical approach would be to mix hard and easy workouts among the three sports. But that leads to an equally untenable proposition: *every day* calls for a hard workout in at least *one* sport. Individual muscle groups may get a break, but the body as a whole never does. And trying to get the proper rotation between the three separate sports is nearly a logistical impossibility: Should you schedule a hard bike and a hard run in the same day? How about a hard swim and a hard run?

Two sport training can be manageable

Two sports a day is perhaps manageable. A duathlete doing two workouts a day could simply trade off between hard/easy runs and hard/easy bike rides. This leads to the "gotta go hard at *something* every single day" problem, but at least it's a rational system, and could be tempered by regularly throwing in total easy days in which *both* workouts are under 70%.

Three sports is another story

But adding the third sport throws a monkey wrench into the works. A triathlete sooner or later begins to get the feeling that her sport is impossible to train properly for. How does an athlete work in long distance aerobic base work, medium-long interval max VO2 work, short interval anaerobic peaking work, plus appropriate recovery, in *three separate sports*, in a seven-day week?

Most experts end up recommending a daily "one and a half workouts" approach: One intense workout in a single sport, and a second, easy workout in a second sport. By rotating regularly through the sports, you end up with a fairly balanced program that most serious competitors can live with.

During my serious triathlon days, I tried all sorts of combinations, including—during one mad season—attempting to train fairly hard in all three sports every day.

A triathlon program has to be "livable"

It took awhile, but I eventually came up with a program that made sense, was "livable," and most importantly, was effective.

Before getting to that, however, let's examine the problem of multi-sport training from the perspective of what we already know about physiology and heart monitor principles.

The first thing we realize is that the primary driving imperative of our running heart monitor program, the preservation of glycogen from workout to workout, has all but disappeared!

That's right, unless you're truly courting disaster by doing two or three sports hard every day, you will generally find that "hitting the wall" in a given discipline is not generally a problem in triathlon training.

The running model makes no sense for triathlons

Why? Because each muscle group is getting enough recovery time between intense workouts to replenish the glycogen burned by the last workout. And because of the principle of muscle specificity, your running muscles are recovering even while you're out wailing on a 50-mile bike ride, and vice versa.

Thus the overriding imperative in our running program of alternating intense days with one or two (or more) sub-70% recovery days now makes no sense.

That's the good news. Hammerheads of the world, rejoice! Those runners (or bikers or swimmers) who genetically cannot make themselves go slower no matter what the coach, the experts, or even their own best judgment tell them, triathlon is the sport for you.

So we don't have to worry about glycogen preservation if we're alternating sports every day, what principles *do* we base our multi-sport training on?

Most principles still apply

Well, everything else still applies. We still need to build an aerobic base, i.e., developing the fat burning capacity of our muscle cells by building dense capillary systems, and the cellular mitochondria and their energy-producing enzymes. The way to accomplish that is *still* longer, slower work. The difference is we no longer need the double benefit of glycogen preservation from the same workout.

We also need to sharpen that aerobic base with VO2 Max workouts, tempo work or longer intervals designed to push our aerobic threshold to higher levels and allow us to operate aerobically at higher and higher levels of performance.

And we need to do anaerobic work—shorter, faster intervals—to train our muscles to deal with and use up the lactic acid that is the inevitable by-product of serious endurance performance.

A Modest Proposal and a Plea For Sanity

This is my proposed solution to the three-sport training conundrum. It's simple, it's rational, and it works. If you are a triathlete who has been driving yourself crazy trying to fit two or three sports (plus job, family, weights, stretching, and god knows what else) into your life, I implore you to try this program for at least a month.

A sane triathlon program

If you are like most triathletes, the biggest problem you'll have with this approach will be your Calvinistic fear that while you are in the midst of doing one thing, you are not also simultaneously doing two others.

Learn to be a bit easier on yourself.

Rotating through the sports, one at a time

The proof of any training scheme ought to be how well it works, not how well it assuages the various psychological pathologies of its practitioners.

So here's the program: *Do a single workout in a single sport per day. Rotate through the sports in sequence so that you end up doing each twice during the week. Take one day off.*

Every week in each sport you will do one aero-bically-oriented workout and one anaerobically-oriented workout (either VO2 Max or peaking, depending on where you are in the season).

Resist the temptation to kill yourself

Gone are the sub-70% recovery workouts. Instead, your aerobic workout will be a long, 75-80% effort. It can be both higher quality and higher quantity workout because we no longer have to be so miserly about glycogen replenishment: you'll have *two full recovery days* before you rotate back to that sport again.

Which is precisely why I'm saying: *Don't try*

to do a daily second workout (unless you're a pro athlete and can dedicate your whole life to getting this right). A second workout in another sport just complicates the recovery scenario for that sport, as well as possibly overburdening the bodily systems that all the sports share (cardiovascular, endocrinal, immunological, etc.).

The second weekly workout in each sport will still be a substantial session, but will be oriented toward more intense efforts; in short, it will be more anaerobic.

Let's take a look at how this plan would affect a frenetic three-sport-per-day program of a good male age-group competitive triathlete who has a PR in an Olympic distance triathlon (1.5K swim, 40K bike, 10K run) of between 2:30 and 2:40.

Tom Trysport, Typical Training Week
BEFORE HM Training

Mon   AM: Run 4 mi. (80-85%)
         PM: Bike 30 mi. (80-85%)
                 Swim 2K intervals (80-85%)

Tue   AM: Swim 1K intervals (80-85%)
         PM: Run 8 mi. (80-85%)
                 Bike 20 mi. (80-85%)

Wed   AM: Bike 10 mi. (80-85%)
         PM: Swim 3K intervals (80-85%)
                 Run 6 mi. (80-85%)

Thu   AM: Run 4 mi. (80-85%)
         PM: Bike 30 mi. (80-85%)
                 Swim 2K intervals (80-85%)

Fri   AM: Swim 1K intervals (80-85%)
         PM: Run 8 mi. (80-85%)
                 Bike 20 mi. (80-85%)

Sat   AM: Bike 10 mi. (80-85%)
         PM: Swim 3K intervals (80-85%)
                 Run 6 mi. (80-85%)

Sun   Rest

Totals: Swim 12K, Bike 120 miles, Run 36 miles
Total number of "hard" days per sport: 6

In this admittedly simplistic scenario, Tom does a good job of rotating through the sports, while emphasizing (with slightly longer distance) only one sport per day, the first portion of his afternoon session. But as with our typical runner's schedule, all of the efforts are in the same general range. There's a good reason for that: going any harder on any particular day would very quickly bring his program crashing down, and going any slower would be unthinkable to a type A+ personality like Tom. In short, he's doing about as much quality and quantity as he can every day. He's probably tired and run down most of the time and his family life is the pits. He has to get up at six every morning to get in his piddling little half-hour work-out, and his two to three-hour afternoon sessions leave him a quivering lump of protoplasm during the part of the evening he manages to stay awake. His rest day on Sunday—which he spends most of sleeping—is the only thing that keeps him going from week to week.

If he were doing the same kind of program in running alone, he would crash and burn in a matter of days, but because he's spreading the trauma out over three sports—two of them non-weight-bearing—he's able to survive from week to week.

But there's no real plan behind Tom's program, no real overload, no real recovery (no yin and yang). Basically, there's no real hard/easy structure in this program; like the typical runner's schedule, it's all semi-hard "training soup." Tom is frantically going through the motions, punching his ticket in all three sports every day, hoping that as a result of all that activity, fitness will just *happen.*

Well, Tom will be in better shape than someone who doesn't train at all (if he doesn't get injured), but he's a long way from getting optimal results for all the effort he's putting in. Plus, he's needlessly neglecting the rest of his life.

Here's how he can get his act together, get in far better shape, and recapture his life and sanity.

Tom Trysport, Typical Training Week
AFTER HM Training

Mon   Bike 45 miles @ 75-80%
Tue   Swim 4K (3K of intervals @80-85%)
Wed   Run 14 mi. @ 75-80%
Thu   Bike 30 miles @80-85%
Fri   Swim 5K @ 75-80%
Sat   Run 12 mi. @ 80-85%
Sun   Rest

Totals: Swim 9K, Bike 75 miles, Run 26 miles
Total number of "hard" days per sport: 2

Training hard and smart

(This is not a complete schedule, of course, just a snapshot of a representative week from the shank of an overall program. He'll need to sharpen up in all three sports with more intense intervals and time trials as he approaches the racing season.)

The difference is that in this plan, Tom is still training hard (around two hours per afternoon), but he is training sensibly. Every day that he's working hard in one sport, he's recovering in the other two. His overall mileage and yardage is lower than it used to be, but mostly what he's given up is truly "junk" miles and yards, i.e., weary rote training performed only out of a misguided sense of discipline, simply because it was written on his schedule.

The other benefits of training sensibly

Now, because he's recovering better and getting more sleep, he's not completely comatose in the evenings and he can actually get to know his family again. He's fresher for his workouts and enjoying the venue changes, instead of frantically trying to cram all the workouts into a day.

And when he races, he'll be delighted to find the minutes dropping off his finish times.

17. Using a Heart Monitor for General Fitness

T he primary emphasis of this book is on using a heart rate monitor for sports performance improvement, a complex subject. Using the same principles for general fitness is a much simpler matter. By and large, you can get excellent health benefits from exercising in the 50 to 60% of max heart rate range.

These benefits include weight control, cardiovascular improvements, lowered blood pressure, and musculo-skeletal strength and flexibility improvements, not to mention the myriad of mental and psychological benefits that have been documented from a regular exercise program.[1]

Health benefits come at 50 to 60% of max

The heart monitor is useful for beginners and fitness enthusiasts in much the same way it is for those hard-headed runners who insist on "training as they feel." Beginners are even less well equipped than runners to judge effort levels, and tend to either under- or overdo their exercise sessions, particularly the very early ones.

The cliché of the on-again-off-again exerciser is a familiar one, and most readers are familiar with the pattern of the well-intentioned exercise program gone bust: starting out with a burst of enthusiasm prompted by a new year, an expensive piece of home gym equipment, or a new love interest, the novitiate huffs and puffs through the first several workouts, gets sore and exhausted, takes a few days off, tries again, pulls a muscle or comes down with a cold, takes a few more days off, and the next thing you know that $2,000 Stride-A-Rama has become a really keen towel rack.

The heart monitor can keep things under control through the initial "breaking in" phase of any exercise program, so that you can get past the early aches, pains and fatigue that often put an immediate end to such a well-intentioned but poorly planned program.

By the same token, the heart monitor can keep the cardiovascularly timid from deluding themselves into thinking that they're getting into shape when they're not. I've seen a lot of folks out strolling along at a slow enough pace to read the date on a lost penny, or peddling a bicycle at a speed designed to do no more than keep the contraption upright. That's fine as far as it goes. I don't want to discourage anyone from doing *any* physical activity, however gentle. After all, there are some benefits to be had from just being outside.

But let's not try to fool ourselves into thinking that anyone is going to get any great benefits from raising your heart rate to 20% of your max. Some fitness professionals might disagree with me, but I think it gives exercise in general a bad name to pretend that great benefits can be reaped by the tamest, most innocuous gesture towards physical movement.

The reason your body gets in shape at all is that it responds to the stress of "overload," which by definition is physical activity more rigorous than that found in the daily routine.

The principle of "overload"

What I'm saying is that the heart monitor can be useful in establishing a "floor" for fitness trainers who might otherwise tend to take warnings about moderation way too seriously. That means that if your program is walking (or cycling), you may need to walk (or cycle) briskly to get into a true "moderate exercise zone," i.e., 50% of your max heart rate.

The big payoff is that this will actually work!

It may seem a bit more rigorous but at least if you adopt a realistic attitude, after three or four weeks on your program you won't need to wonder why your weight didn't drop, your blood pressure stayed the same, and you don't feel 20 years younger, contrary to all the exercise hoopla you've read or heard.

Let's take a sample case. Gladys Golightly is a 45-year-old, slightly overweight, sedentary housewife who hasn't done much of anything physical since she stopped playing tennis in her 20's. Her blood pressure has gotten high enough that her doctor has told her (twice now!) that she needs to start getting some exercise.

Our Max HR formula (from page 4) would predict her max to be about 183 (205 minus half her age), and let's say she's been to her doctor to get checked out and had a treadmill stress test that confirmed that max.

The Karvonen method is probably the way to go

Using the Karvonen method, her 50-60% range would be 129 to 140 beats per minute. As you can see, the Karvonen method presents a much more rigorous (and I would argue, a much more realistic) target than the straight percentage method, which gives 90-110.

An extreme case like this, in fact, demonstrates the efficacy of the Karvonen method. Telling Gladys she can get good exercise benefits by getting her heart rate up to 90 amounts to a hoax. With a resting rate of 75, she probably raises her heart rate 15 beats just getting out of her easy chair. No doubt she can get *some* benefits from raising her heart rate to 90, but then again, you can probably get *some* health benefits from simply breathing more deeply.

So let's not try to pull the wool over Gladys's eyes. We need to get her on a program that's going to have her heart rate well into the triple digits for her to get the kind of wonderful, life-changing rewards she's always been told she could get from an exercise program.

A realistic training zone will yield real results

Early exercise promoters like Dr. Kenneth Cooper have recommended minimal basic programs of 20 minutes of aerobic activity three times a week.[2] I'd like to suggest that a daily or near-daily program is better in the long run, for the simple reason that it can quickly become habitual and ingrained into a healthy lifestyle, whereas a schedule of less than every other day may soon be skipped, then forgotten for periods of time, and then finally abandoned. The four-week program that follows intersperses both "rest days" and "easy days" in the early going, but then begins eliminating them as progress is made toward fitness.

A near-daily program is best

The activity you choose almost doesn't matter. Certainly walking is an excellent choice and offers the same convenience and simplicity as running, but without the associated risks of injury and over-training.

Choosing your activity

A truly excellent program would incorporate several different activities in rotation: walking one day, Life Cycling the next, perhaps swimming or aerobics class on the third, etc. The advantages of the strength and flexibility improvements with different muscles groups would be considerable.

More than one is even better!

But the most important factor by far is the cardiovascular benefits to be derived from 15 to 30 minutes spent at 50 to 60% of maximum heart rate. The program outlined below is designed to build up slowly to that point, but in the early going using some segments at lesser effort (30-40% of max) as warm-ups, cooldowns and "easy days."

Before starting the program, you should follow these steps. Then get going on Week 1 to start building a solid, all around fitness program using a heart monitor:

3 Steps to get started

1. Get your doctor to check you out and give you an OK to start an exercise program.

2. Get a treadmill stress test to determine your Maximum Heart Rate.

3. Work out your Heart Rate Training Chart on page 33 to determine your 50-60% fitness training zone.

4. Start on Week 1 and have fun!

4 Week Fitness Program—Week 1

Fitness:

WEEK 1

Mon	10 minutes in 30-40% zone 5 minutes in 50-60% zone 5 minutes in 30-40% zone
Tue	10 minutes in 30-40% zone
Wed	10 minutes in 30-40% zone 5 minutes in 50-60% zone 5 minutes in 30-40% zone
Thu	Rest
Fri	10 minutes in 30-40% zone 5 minutes in 50-60% zone 5 minutes in 30-40% zone
Sat	Rest
Sun	Rest

Total time in 30-40% Zone: 55
Total time in 50-60% Zone: 15

4 Week Fitness Program—Week 2

Mon	10 minutes in 30-40% zone 10 minutes in 50-60% zone 10 minutes in 30-40% zone
Tue	15 minutes in 30-40% zone
Wed	10 minutes in 30-40% zone 10 minutes in 50-60% zone 10 minutes in 30-40% zone
Thu	15 minutes in 30-40% zone
Fri	10 minutes in 30-40% zone 5 minutes in 50-60% zone 5 minutes in 30-40% zone
Sat	Rest
Sun	Rest

Total time in 30-40% Zone: 85
Total time in 50-60% Zone: 25

4 Week Fitness Program—Week 3

Fitness:

WEEK 3

Mon   10 minutes in 30-40% zone
15 minutes in 50-60% zone
10 minutes in 30-40% zone

Tue   20 minutes in 30-40% zone

Wed   10 minutes in 30-40% zone
15 minutes in 50-60% zone
10 minutes in 30-40% zone

Thu   20 minutes in 30-40% zone

Fri   10 minutes in 30-40% zone
15 minutes in 50-60% zone
5 minutes in 30-40% zone

Sat   Rest

Sun   20 minutes in 30-40% zone

Total time in 30-40% Zone: 105
Total time in 50-60% Zone: 45

4 Week Fitness Program—Week 4

Fitness:

WEEK 4

Mon   10 minutes in 30-40% zone
        20 minutes in 50-60% zone
        5 minutes in 30-40% zone

Tue   30 minutes in 30-40% zone

Wed   10 minutes in 30-40% zone
        20 minutes in 50-60% zone
        5 minutes in 30-40% zone

Thu   30 minutes in 30-40% zone

Fri   10 minutes in 30-40% zone
        20 minutes in 50-60% zone
        5 minutes in 30-40% zone

Sat   30 minutes in 30-40% zone

Sun   30 minutes in 30-40% zone

Total time in 30-40% Zone: 165
Total time in 50-60% Zone: 60

*Adjusting
the
intensity*

This program can be gradually adjusted upward in intensity as the trainer becomes fitter. The goal should be to increase effort and frequency until the subject is spending between 20 and 40 minutes per day in the 50-60% range, with one or two "easy days" at 30-40% of max (or days off) as needed.

The key thing is to make the program a part of your daily life, to stick with it and increase the effort gradually. The results you'll see within a week or two will thrill you. And if you keep it up for several months, you'll be glowing with good health. The heart monitor guarantees your success!

Appendix

A. How to Set Up a Training Chart Spreadsheet

This simple spreadsheet format will yield a "Karvonen Method" Training Effort Chart. Enter your Actual Max Heart Rate in cell A1, your Morning Resting Heart Rate in cell A2, then type in the formulas as shown in cells B4 through B20.

	A	B
1	Actual Max HR	
2	Resting HR	
3		
4	100% =	=A1
5	95%=	=.95*(A1-A2) + A2
6	90%=	=.90*(A1-A2) + A2
7	85%=	=.85*(A1-A2) + A2
8	80%=	=.80*(A1-A2) + A2
9	75%=	=.75*(A1-A2) + A2
10	70%=	=.70*(A1-A2) + A2
11	65%=	=.65*(A1-A2) + A2
12	60%=	=.60*(A1-A2) + A2
13	55%=	=.55*(A1-A2) + A2
14	45%=	=.45*(A1-A2) + A2
15	40%=	=.40*(A1-A2) + A2
16	35%=	=.35*(A1-A2) + A2
17	30%=	=.30*(A1-A2) + A2
18	25%=	=.25*(A1-A2) + A2
19	20%=	=.20*(A1-A2) + A2
20	15%=	=.15*(A1-A2) + A2

B. An Overview of Training Theory and the Concept of Periodization

by John L. Parker, Jr.

(Adapted from *Guide for the Elite Runner*, by John L. Parker, Jr. and Marty Liquori, Seaview Books, 1980)

Of Gurus and Madmen: a Quick History

One point to be made at the outset of any discussion of the evolution of training methods: Elite distance runners have tended to be the most fiercely independent of almost all athletes. They necessarily spend many hours in introspection, analyzing their reactions to physical stress. They generally tend to think they know more about their bodies than anyone else. Over the years, history has shown that the best ones were often right.

Many successful runners have been self-coached, perhaps with informal advice on training matters from trusted but not dominating coaches. This was true of Zatopek in the 1950s, of Bannister in 1954 when he ran the first sub-four-minute mile, and of New Zealand's great 3:49 miler, John Walker (though Bannister occasionally consulted with Franz Stampfl and Walker relied regularly on Arch Jelly).

It is not that good runners don't want or need coaches; indeed, history has shown that a certain type of coach is actually sought out by runners in search of the most advanced training wisdom. Such coaches often exhibit dynamic personalities and undeniable qualities of salesmanship (Marty Liquori's college coach, Jumbo Elliot of Villanova, comes to mind).

Such men have, first and foremost, an ability to make athletes believe in themselves and their training. Over the decades several of these men have distinguished themselves by their innovative approaches to training, and by the manner in which they seemed to motivate their athletes through sheer charisma.

All too often, however, great athletes have found themselves at a point at which they felt they knew more intuitively about their own bodies and training than the coach did from even the most careful observation and the most wide-ranging experience.

Because the most famous running coaches have tended to be "cock o' the walk" types, stern father figures, or unabashed gurus, they have brooked no nonsense. As a result, unpleasant impasses resulted. Ill feelings occasionally became lengthy imbroglios. Peter Snell reached such a point with Arthur Lydiard in the years between his remarkable gold medal Olympiads in Rome and Tokyo, but the two were able to patch things up at the last minute, Lydiard worrying all the while that perhaps it was "too late" for him to "salvage" poor Snell's condition. Snell managed quite well, thank you, winning the gold at both 800 and 1,500 meters. But the point is that the reader should approach the pontifications of the great distance coaches with, at the very least, a grain of salt.

Much of running is mental, and the guru-coaches (particularly Cerutty of Australia, Lydiard of New Zealand, and the Americans Jumbo Elliot of Villanova and Bill Bowerman of Oregon) probably have been successful more because they knew how to harness a runner's heart and mind than because of any mysterious secret training formula.

Each of the great coaches has, after all, held an occasional silly idea or two over the years (some still do), but the line between stubbornness and tenacity is often ambiguous. These coaches sensed that much of their athletes' confidence derived from the fact that the teacher never lacked an opinion on any matter, no matter how trivial or by what circuitous logic he reached his conclusion. A fictitious example: "Salt tablets? No, a runner should never take pure salt tablets. You never find salt tablets in nature, do you? Therefore, they must be unnatural." That sort of thing.

Over the past several decades first one guru-coach, then another (with an occasional mad doctor-coach), has reigned as the all-knowing, all-seeing Oz of Endurance Sports. With the undeniable accomplishments of their great athletes in their back pockets, at least these guru coaches have been experts with portfolio. (We needn't even discuss those other individuals who would claim our attention because they've published a book or because they happen to be a chiropractor who jogs.)

Even the great Lydiard is not without off-the-wall ideas. For example, he says the following about training in the heat: "In high temperatures, it's possible to continue steady running for an hour or more, even when the thermometer is near 100 degrees. But the humidity must also be high, so that the moisture perspired remains on the skin surface to assist with cooling. If the humidity is low and the perspiration evaporates quickly, you'll suffer from dehydration and have difficulty."

The New Zealand coach claims to have proved his "train in the humidity" theory by personal trial. But it shows a profound misunderstanding of human physiology and the mechanics of perspiration.

Although it is true that there is a danger of dehydration on hot dry days, a hot humid day presents an equal or greater danger. Perspiration cools the body only when it evaporates, taking away the heat with the escaping molecules. The fact that the body is covered with sweat on a hot humid day merely means the pores are producing more perspiration than will readily evaporate, and thus the runner's natural cooling system is overloaded.

It is, in fact, much easier to train in a dry warm climate than a humid warm climate. Of course, precautions against dehydration should be taken. Experience has shown, however, that the runner will more readily recognize the symptoms of dehydration (dizziness, parched mouth, etc.), whereas heat prostration and stroke give much less warning to the inexperienced competitor and thus pose far greater threats to physical well-being.

Still, Lydiard has demonstrated a self-effacement rarely seen in great coaches. Unlike many, he is willing to admit that a theory he has held has been shown to be incorrect, but that hasn't happened often.

They have been and are great men, the Elliots, the Iglois, the Ceruttys, and the Lydiards. They have contributed much to the sport and are part of its history. They have been colorful, delightful, witty, and life-giving. They have also occasionally been wrong.

But that is not to take anything away from them. They were

often operating on intuition, hunch, and trial and error. The study of exercise physiology is only now beginning to dovetail with the philosophies of the guru-coaches and the innovative self-coached runners. As it does, what is truly amazing about those energetic, dedicated men is not that they were occasionally wrong but that they were so right about so many things without really knowing why.

Workouts: From Lazy Afternoons to Lydiard

Training theory began changing radically in the 1950s. Before that, many coaches thought that hard training would "tire" an athlete out; workouts were light and the natural aerobic athlete triumphed by sheer luck of the genetic dice.

A miler's afternoon used to include some light jogging, a set of calisthenics, a few wind sprints, and a vigorous rubdown. An athlete might be considered something more (or less) than human if he covered more than two or three miles in a day.

On the other hand, around the turn of the century, before Mr. Ford's tin Lizzie, people walked a great deal more; there was more horseback riding, and more physical labor in general, which probably helps to explain why runners in those early days were able to achieve even the relatively modest accomplishments they did. A professional runner at the turn of the century named Walter Goodall George ran a 4:12.8 mile, which is still a respectable clocking (albeit more befitting a high school performer these days). Pre-1900 training theory consisted of a blend of half truths and superstitions. Much was made of massages, avoidance of the company of ladies, the evils of cigars, and not over-tiring oneself. Still and all, George's 4:12 stood as the record for a full 30 years, and it certainly indicates that whatever natural gifts he may have been born with, he and his trainers must have stumbled on a system that entailed some good hard work.

The Scientists

Before the interval era was ushered in by Emil Zatopek in the early 1950s, distance runners generally trained solely by running longish distances (usually 4 to 12 miles) at relatively slow paces. The reasoning was that if one's race was the 6-mile distance, one should train by running 12 miles half as fast. Besides, in those days, no one really knew what the limits of human endurance were, much less how much time was needed to recuperate after venturing farther and farther into those strange and frightening valleys of fatigue.

The Scandinavians enjoyed preeminence in the 1940s with their fartlek system, and in 1944 the Swede Arne Andersson lowered the mile record to 4:01.6, which surely demonstrated the need for speed as well as endurance training.

But with Zatopek came the curious notion that one could run, on a consistent and organized basis, very hard, very short, and very many training runs, and thus accustom oneself to running a long race at a faster pace. Or, as the irrepressible Zatopek then said: "I already know how to run slow. I want to learn how to run fast." The world-renowned Czech was a charismatic figure; running as he did with a rolling head and an agonized expression on his face, he was hard to miss on the track. Off the track he made news as well. Once when he was frisking around with his wife, a javelin thrower, he tossed her into a stream and was dismayed to find out she had broken her ankle. For weeks thereafter, Zatopek insisted on carrying her on his back during his runs through the forest. He did so until his doctor insisted he stop. It was entirely proper that such a man would discover a system of training that would revolutionize distance running and bring about records undreamed of in earlier times. Zatopek won an unprecedented trio of gold medals in the 1952 Helsinki Olympics.

The interval technique had immediate appeal for the scientifically minded German coaches and theorists; after all, a measured track is much more like a laboratory than the trails or roads. The distances are exact, and the stopwatch tells no lies.

Runners could be put through their paces like so many rats on a wheel; the times were religiously recorded, studied, and filed away for future reference. It fascinated a lot of people, particularly coaches who had long suspected that runners out of observation range on a cross-country course were probably loafing. Interval training kept everyone under the microscope's eye on the track, and no one could ever hide from the cruelty of the unsympathetic stopwatch. And it also was great fun playing around with the formulas on paper: 12 X 330 @ 42 w/ 110j. That sounds like a fine afternoon's entertainment for the boys.

Then someone developed the more elaborate "stepdowns": 1 X mile @4:30 w/440j, 2 X 880 @2:10 w/220j, 4 X 440 @ 77 w/110j, and so on. A coach could spend a morning tinkering with such formulas and almost feel as if he had had a workout himself.

It was marvelous! An entire season's workouts could be kept on a few three-by-five cards. Soon after Zatopek retired, everyone was interval-crazy. People were doing intervals in the morning, intervals in the afternoon. Not many observers seemed to notice the figurative corpses strewn along the way, burned out by the mind-ragging routine which strict interval training necessarily becomes. To this day in the US there are thousands of former high school athletes who lived through it all and who still sneer openly when a modern-day jogger goes by. They are casualties of the interval system and they no longer want any part of running. Who can blame them? To them running meant nothing more than endless days of lung-searing 440's and 330's under the scrutiny of a record-keeping tyrant.

But there were some very convincing results brought about by the tough-minded souls who thrived under such pressure. Zatopek, the Englishman Gordon Pirie, the Russian Vladimir Kuts, the American miler Jim Beatty, and many, many more used the interval method to make big names for themselves while exploring new dimensions of endurance in the human animal. It appeared that the training riddle was on the verge of being solved once and for all: One had only to juggle the little numbers until the right formula was reached, then just sit back and wait for the gold medals to roll in.

Roger Bannister, a young British medical student, made the biggest breakthrough of them all. His interval-training technique was simplicity itself: Run ten quarter-miles in under 60 seconds with a short (two minute) rest. If one could do that, surely one could put four such quarter-miles together on race day and the first four-minute mile would be accomplished.

In the early spring of 1954, he had finally reduced his average time in the ten-quarter workout from 66 to 59 seconds each. Three weeks later, on May 6, 1954, in a well-planned, well-executed assault on an old barrier, Roger Bannister became the first human to run a mile in less than four minutes.

The Aussies

Soon thereafter, a young man in Australia named John Landy began running even faster. His training was said to be as fierce as any yet attempted, with the possible exception of that of Zatopek. Why, Landy was reputed to run as much as 50 miles a week!

By sheer force of his ebullient personality, his coach, Percy Cerutty, was coaxing the runners at his primitive seaside camp, Portsea, to reach the outer limit of their endurance. No scientific recorder of 440 times was Percy; he believed training should be basically an emotional, joyful, and painful experience. His runners (and Percy too), ran long hard distances, swam in the rugged surf, lifted heavy weights, and drove themselves relentlessly up and down the steep, sandy hill known as "Agony."

Such training within a few years produced an athlete such as the world had never seen before. Both strong and fast, fearless in training as well as racing, he swept all before him. His name was Herb Elliot and he ran times for the mile in the early sixties that would still be respectable today (3:55 and under)

Lydiard and the Kiwis

But soon another set of athletes from "down under," along with their equally captivating coach, were having their say. Marathoner Arthur Lydiard had experimented on his own body for years to find the best approach to physical conditioning. He ran 100 miles a week, he ran 200 miles a week, he ran *more* than 200 miles a week. Slowly his training theories evolved. He used them successfully in his own races, winning national titles in the marathon despite the fact that he was approaching middle age. Soon he was being sought out for training advice.

With the consistent successes of runners like Murray Halberg in the 5000 meters and Peter Snell in the 800 and 1500, as well as several internationally successful marathoners, Lydiard established himself as *the* training theorist of the modern era. Nearly every knowledgeable coach today, whether he acknowledges it or not, uses some form of the Lydiard system.

The original Lydiard system was divided into three distinct phases: marathon training, hill training, and speed training.

The marathon stage was extremely important, serving as the "base" for all future work, the foundation for the elaborate building to be constructed later. Although Lydiard did not know exactly *why* such a phase was important, he did understand that it was the first step toward superior conditioning. From a scientific point of view, we now know that his long hard runs (on the border between aerobic and anaerobic pace) were developing the cellular and capillary capacities of his athletes for the arduous tasks ahead. This phase was to last four months. The length of the runs varied during the week, and light jogging generally made the morning workout a recovery time.

The centerpiece of this type of training was the daily long afternoon run, along with the Sunday 20-plus-miler. The goal was to get in 100 aerobic miles in addition to some light morning jogging.

The second phase (hill training) Lydiard thought of as merely a bridge between the long runs and the much quicker running required on the track. He therefore had his runners "spring" up hills of varying inclines before gently descending by a longer route, forming a more or less continuous circuit, the idea being to build the strength of the leg muscles and to develop the racing stride. It is this phase of Lydiard's system which is probably the most controversial and also the most easily dispensed with. Hill training puts a great deal of strain on muscles and tendons, and while it is good hard anaerobic work, it must be done correctly and at the right time of year in order to avoid injuries. Many elite runners ignore the true hill-training phase altogether except to see that they have plenty of inclines on their longer courses. Very few runners who do hill work actually do it as Lydiard suggests, using the slow, springing stride.

The final phase in Lydiard's system was the interval "sharpening" period, during which the runner's racing endurance would be honed to a fine edge. In Lydiard's mind, the whole point of the training cycle was to "bring around" a runner at the right time, which, as observers of the "Olympic letdown" phenomenon know, is not as easy as it sounds.

After a runner completed the interval phase, Lydiard considered him to be fully conditioned and ready to race for the whole competitive season with no further hard work. Lydiard assumed that the races themselves would further sharpen the athlete and thus he counseled that his runners only jog lightly between competitions.

When his race performances began to drop off, Lydiard figured the runner had pretty much drawn out all the capital he had deposited in his fitness bank account and it was time to go home. A rest would be followed by a new base-building phase.

As with others who develop breakthrough methods, the successes of his athletes showed just how well the Lydiard system could prepare an athlete to compete. Within hours of each other, two of his athletes took gold medals in the 1960 Rome Olympics: Snell in the 800 meters, Halberg in the 5,000. Later, teammate Barry Magee added a bronze in the marathon. Tiny New Zealand—all but unheard of since the days of world-record holder Jack Lovelock of the 1930s—had once again become a dominant force in distance-running circles.

The Current Era

Modern coaches and self-coached runners have tinkered with and refined Lydiard's methods, but the overall philosophy has remained intact. Ron Clarke, the great Australian distance runner of the middle and late 1960s, quit running altogether when he was a teenager, a typical "burnout" from rigid interval training. He got interested again in his twenties because he found marathon training more mentally acceptable.

It wasn't until Arthur Lydiard suggested to him that he needed both a base of distance *and* a sharpening interval process, however, that Ron Clarke began smashing world records by incredible margins. Although he had little success in tactical races in the Olympics, Clarke's front-running record performances were so astounding that many experts still regard him as the greatest distance runner ever. For example, on December 18, 1963, Clarke broke the six-year-old 6-mile world record by *36 seconds* when he ran 27:17.6 in Melbourne. His 10,000-meter best of 27:39.4 is to this day a competitive mark, though he retired in 1969.

Jim Ryun's high school (and later college) coach Bob Timmons, used much of the Lydiard method in developing his great prodigy, the first high school four-minute miler and later the world record holder (at 3:51.3 and 3:51.1).

Lasse Viren's coach, Rolf Haikkola, said that he blends Lydiard's long aerobic runs with Igloi's surge training, Cerutty's hill training, and Paavo Nurmi's steady "pace running" (actually just interval training using longer distances).

Many modern athletes such as Frank Shorter and Bill Rodgers have pretty much disregarded Lydiard's idea of building to racing shape only to slacken off completely during the competitive season. Runners as compulsive as they are probably couldn't handle the relative inactivity of a pure "racing season," and thus they remained active year around during their competitive days. Obviously they tapered off before big races, and they also planned periods of rest and easy running after hard racing seasons in order to give themselves a mental and physical break.

Shorter's 140-mile-per-week training was uncomplicated: overdistance every morning (seven to ten miles at an easy pace), either a long run or else an interval session (of which he ran two per week) in the afternoon, and a 20-miler on Sunday. Not much different than Lydiard's athletes in the 1960s.

Perhaps someone will come along with some new breakthrough concept and we'll see another round of world records by his or her athletes, but it doesn't seem likely.

Lydiard, through trial and error, stumbled onto training ideas that mesh well with current physiological research. There is a need for a base of long endurance runs because mitochondrial and capillary development cannot be as efficiently accomplished in any other way; there is a need to "sharpen" an athlete by interval training, perfecting the anaerobic pathways and training the muscles to survive and dispose of the lactic acid necessarily generated at racing paces.

It is therefore not surprising that Lydiard's basic theories are still intact long after his original batch of great runners have hung up their famous black racing vests with the silver fern on the breast.

Lasse Viren, one of the greatest runners ever, owes no more to his own coach than he does to Lydiard. It was Lydiard, in fact, who was hired by the Finnish government in 1966 to revamp the flagging national training program, and it was the program he helped establish that subsequently produced the great new Flying Finn. Thus when Lydiard claims credit for most modern running theory, he is not far off the mark.

The training methods of Sebastian Coe, a world record holder in the mile at 3:49 flat, are basically those of the New Zealand coach, as are those of the former record holder and fellow New Zealander John Walker, who is, for the most part, self-coached.

With the possible exception of the heart monitor, the innovations in endurance training during the past decades have been minor in comparison to Lydiard's. Altitude training, carbohydrate loading, blood reinfusion, electrolyte drinks, megavitamins, vegetarianism, bee pollen, and the $100 training shoe all indicate that, as far as basic training concepts go, the great Kiwi coach pretty much led us to the top of the mountain.

Periodization

One facet implicit in Lydiard's program—as well as many other past and present coaches—is the idea of training "seasons." Fall (in the northern hemisphere, anyway) has always been cross country season, a time to run a lot of miles over hill and dale in order to generally improve conditioning for shorter, faster races on the track later. Over the winter, the runner might take a short break or perhaps run a few indoor races to tune up for the upcoming track season.

Spring would find the runner on the track, beginning to work more intensely with tempo pace work, hard intervals, and speed work, all in preparation for the serious racing in late spring and early summer.

Most champion endurance athletes and their coaches have understood intuitively that they would not be able to produce peak performances—the kind that win championships and set records—at will. Such ultimate efforts would only come as a result of a conscientiously maintained pattern of strength, stamina, speed, and rest, repeated over and over for a number of years. And by "rest" I don't mean a weekend off. I mean several weeks or months composed of various mixtures of complete rest, very light training and cross-training. Such a period allows the body to heal up, and to internalize and integrate the training of the previous season. No small part of this process is mental and perhaps spritual, as the athlete allows his or her mind to "go fallow," all the better to rejuvenate the competitive will and spirit the endurance athlete must daily call upon to train successfully.

These days those of us no longer in a scholastic setting tend to forget the idea of "seasons." When road races of varying distances—as well as triathlons, bike races, walkathons, kayak derbies, you name it—are accessible to most of us every weekend, it's all too easy to get caught up in the whirl of regular competition and to forget about the ebb and flow pattern our bodies need to accomplish truly difficult tasks.

Elite American marathoners and track distance runners have justly received a great deal of criticism over the past several decades for succumbing to the siren song (as well siren paycheck) of the weekly road race. Implicit in this criticism is a simple truism of endurance sports: You cannot achieve your ultimate potential while attempting to compete on a year around basis, i.e., when your entire calendar year becomes one long racing season.

What holds true for elite competitive athletes is also true for middle and back of the packers: Attempting to train and race at the same level all the time is a sure formula for overtraining, burnout, and general mediocrity.

The solution for those of us no longer in school is to make our own seasons. Pick key races at different times of the year, decide on some achievable but slightly daunting goal performances for those races, and then sketch out a realistic program to accomplish your dreams.

Then take a breather. Play some tennis, go on some hikes, whatever. Get your head together and give your poor knees and quads a break. Then, when you're feeling refreshed, strong, and itchy to get back to it, go on to the next buildup.

Your Own Training: A Realistic Approach

A good basic approach to training can be succinctly stated as follows: Develop a base by running mostly longer, aerobic runs. Then begin interspersing several more intense sessions per week, either tempo runs or interval workouts. These interval workouts should be of varying distances, from 200 meters up to one mile runs, and in the early part of the buildup should reach 85 to 90% of max HR, but later get much sharper (95-100%) as the athlete approaches a targeted race. The recovery interval should be anywhere from one-half to 100% of the distance of the repetition, and will generally be in the form of jogging.

The 12-week programs included in this book follow this approach and can be used (with some modifications) by most athletes to set up a program to peak for a goal race.

Every level of these 12-week plans start with mostly longer aerobic runs, and begin integrating one aerobic threshold and one lactate training session per week.

Of course there are more elaborate ways of going about it. Some coaches would have you do months of nothing but long, slow running before beginning any intensity. Some would insist, as Lydiard does, on a season of hill training between the base phase and the interval phase.

What I've tried to do is come up with an overall approach that most athletes can live with, an approach that won't either bore them to death or burn them out in a month.

The programs are simple, but they aren't easy. It takes discipline to follow a careful plan patiently and allow the results to come naturally. It's not a good idea to skip from Week 3 to Week 8, for instance. It's not a good idea to do an extra set of 400 meter intervals, thinking that you can shortcut the process. It's not a good idea to run an all-out race in the middle of your buildup.

And, as always: You really do need to do recovery runs under 70% if you expect to do the tempo runs and intervals at the appropriate intensity.

If you go about it carefully and with patience, doing two or three 12-week buildups per year, each followed by a sufficient fallow period of rest and play, I have no doubt whatsoever that you can achieve performances you previously only dreamed of.

Selection Chart–Choose Your Level
(use weekly mileage unless you're a veteran runner
starting from scratch)

	Weekly Mileage	5K PR	10K PR
Novice	10-20	25:00-30:00	55:00-65:00
Intermediate	20-30	23:00-25:00	50:00-55:00
Advanced	30-40	20:00-23:00	45:00-50:00
Competitive	40-50	18:00-20:00	38:00-45:00

C. Starting from Scratch: a 4-week schedule

These schedules are to be used by runners who have been out of active training for a month or more. They are designed to get the athlete "in shape to train" by developing fitness at a gentle, steady rate, with plenty of rest in the early going.

To determine which level would be most appropriate for you, use either your PRs at 5K or 10K, or use your normal weekly mileage *when you are training well and* the table on page 230 (it's the same one we used in Chapter 14). Start out with the appropriate "Starting from Scratch" program below, but be prepared to shift to a harder or easier one, depending on how easily you adapt to the program.

Runners whose training was interrupted for only a few weeks may find that a week or two of this rehabilitative training is all that's needed before beginning their 12-Week program as outlined in Chapter 14.

4 Week Scratch Program—Novice—Week 1

NOVICE:

WEEK 1

		Total Miles
Monday	3 Miles <70%	3
Tuesday	3 Miles <70%	3
Wednesday	OFF	0
Thursday	3 Miles <70%	3
Friday	3 Miles <70%	3
Saturday	OFF	0
Sunday	OFF	0

Weekly Mileage	12
Hard Days	0

4 Week Scratch Program—Novice—Week 2

NOVICE:

WEEK 2

		Total Miles
Monday	3 Miles <70%	3
Tuesday	4 Miles <70%	4
Wednesday	OFF	0
Thursday	3 Miles <70%	3
Friday	4 Miles <70%	4
Saturday	OFF	0
Sunday	OFF	0

Weekly Mileage	14
Hard Days	0

4 Week Scratch Program—Novice—Week 3

NOVICE:

WEEK 3

		Total Miles
Monday	3 Miles <70%	3
Tuesday	4 Miles <70%	3
Wednesday	OFF	0
Thursday	3 Miles <70%	3
Friday	4 Miles <70%	4
Saturday	OFF	0
Sunday	3 Miles <70%	3

Weekly Mileage	16
Hard Days	0

4 Week Scratch Program—Novice—Week 4

NOVICE:

WEEK 4

		Total Miles
Monday	3 Miles <70%	3
Tuesday	4 Miles <70%	3
Wednesday	OFF	0
Thursday	3 Miles <70%	3
Friday	4 Miles <70%	4
Saturday	OFF	0
Sunday	3 Miles <70%	4

Weekly/Monthly Mileage	17/59
Hard Days	0

4 Week Scratch—Intermediate—Week 1

Intermediate:

WEEK 1

		Total Miles
Monday	3 Miles <70%	3
Tuesday	4 Miles <70%	4
Wednesday	OFF	0
Thursday	3 Miles <70%	3
Friday	4 Miles <70%	4
Saturday	OFF	0
Sunday	OFF	0

Weekly Mileage	14
Hard Days	0

4 Week Scratch—Intermediate—Week 2

Intermediate:

WEEK 2

		Total Miles
Monday	4 Miles <70%	4
Tuesday	4 Miles <70%	4
Wednesday	OFF	0
Thursday	4 Miles <70%	4
Friday	4 Miles <70%	4
Saturday	OFF	0
Sunday	OFF	0

Weekly Mileage	16
Hard Days	0

4 Week Scratch—Intermediate—Week 3

Intermediate:

WEEK 3

		Total Miles
Monday	4 Miles <70%	4
Tuesday	5 Miles <70%	5
Wednesday	OFF	0
Thursday	4 Miles <70%	4
Friday	5 Miles <70%	5
Saturday	OFF	0
Sunday	3 Miles <70%	3

Weekly Mileage	21
Hard Days	0

4 Week Scratch—Intermediate—Week 4

Intermediate:

WEEK 4

		Total Miles
Monday	5 Miles <70%	5
Tuesday	5 Miles <70%	5
Wednesday	OFF	0
Thursday	5 Miles <70%	5
Friday	5 Miles <70%	5
Saturday	OFF	0
Sunday	3 Miles <70%	3

Weekly/Monthly Mileage	23/74
Hard Days	0

4 Week Scratch—Advanced—Week 1

Advanced:

WEEK 1

		Total Miles
Monday	4 Miles <70%	4
Tuesday	4 Miles <70%	4
Wednesday	OFF	0
Thursday	4 Miles <70%	4
Friday	4 Miles <70%	4
Saturday	OFF	0
Sunday	OFF	0

Weekly Mileage	16
Hard Days	0

4 Week Scratch—Advanced—Week 2

Advanced:

WEEK 2

		Total Miles
Monday	5 Miles <70%	5
Tuesday	4 Miles <70%	4
Wednesday	OFF	0
Thursday	5 Miles <70%	5
Friday	4 Miles <70%	4
Saturday	OFF	0
Sunday	OFF	0

Weekly Mileage	18
Hard Days	0

4 Week Scratch—Advanced—Week 3

Advanced:
WEEK 3

		Total Miles
Monday	5 Miles <70%	5
Tuesday	5 Miles <70%	5
Wednesday	OFF	0
Thursday	5 Miles <70%	5
Friday	5 Miles <70%	5
Saturday	OFF	0
Sunday	4 Miles <70%	4

Weekly Mileage	24
Hard Days	0

4 Week Scratch—Advanced—Week 4

Advanced:

WEEK 4

		Total Miles
Monday	5 Miles <70%	5
Tuesday	6 Miles <70%	6
Wednesday	OFF	0
Thursday	5 Miles <70%	5
Friday	6 Miles <70%	6
Saturday	OFF	0
Sunday	5 Miles <70%	5

Weekly/Monthly Mileage	27/85
Hard Days	0

4 Week Scratch—Competitive—Week 1

Competitive:

WEEK 1

		Total Miles
Monday	4 Miles <70%	4
Tuesday	5 Miles <70%	5
Wednesday	OFF	0
Thursday	4 Miles <70%	4
Friday	5 Miles <70%	5
Saturday	OFF	0
Sunday	OFF	0

Weekly Mileage	18
Hard Days	0

4 Week Scratch—Competitive—Week 2

Competitive:

WEEK 2

		Total Miles
Monday	5 Miles <70%	5
Tuesday	5 Miles <70%	5
Wednesday	OFF	0
Thursday	5 Miles <70%	5
Friday	5 Miles <70%	5
Saturday	OFF	0
Sunday	4 Miles <70%	4

Weekly Mileage 24
Hard Days 0

4 Week Scratch—Competitive—Week 3

Competitive:

WEEK 3

		Total Miles
Monday	5 Miles <70%	5
Tuesday	5 Miles <70%	5
Wednesday	3 Miles <70%	3
Thursday	5 Miles <70%	5
Friday	5 Miles <70%	5
Saturday	5 Miles <70%	5
Sunday	OFF	0

Weekly Mileage	28
Hard Days	0

4 Week Scratch—Competitive—Week 4

Competitive:

WEEK 4

		Total Miles
Monday	6 Miles <70%	6
Tuesday	7 Miles <70%	7
Wednesday	3 Miles <70%	3
Thursday	6 Miles <70%	6
Friday	7 Miles <70%	7
Saturday	OFF	0
Sunday	6 Miles <70%	6

Weekly/Monthly Mileage	35/105
Hard Days	0

Footnotes

Chapter 1
1. The widely cited formula, 220 – age, (see Galloway, Jeff, *Galloway's Book on Running*, Shelter Publications, Inc., 1984, p. 33) has been shown to be inaccurate for a "chronically fit" population, such as endurance athletes. See Benson, Roy, *The Runner's Coach*, Cedarwinds, 1995, p. 10.
2. Wilmore, Jack, and Costill, David. *Physiology of Sport and Exercise*, Human Kinetics, 1994, p. 521.

Chapter 4
1. Wilmore and Costill, p. 221.
2. Ibid., pp. 221-222.
3. Ibid., pp. 221-222.
4. Edwards, Sally, *The Heart Rate Monitor Book*, Polar Electro, Inc., NY, 1993, p. 44.
5. Benson, p. 9

Chapter 5
1. Wilmore and Costill, pg 177.

Chapter 7
1. See, for instance, Parker, John L. and Liquori, Marty, *Guide for the Elite Runner*, Seaview Books, NY, 1980, p. 75; also: Galloway, p. 39; Noakes, Tim, *Lore of Running*, Human Kinetics, Champaign, IL, 1991, pp. 154-155, 188
2. Parker, John L., *Runners and Other Dreamers*, Cedarwinds Publishing, 1989, pg 203
3. Ibid., p. 177

Chapter 9
1. Galloway, pp. 43-44

Chapter 10
1. Moore, Kenny, "Watching Their Steps," *Sports Illustrated*,

May 3, 1973, p. 84.

2. Moore, p. 83. The reason that results are sometimes confusing is that occasionally the laboratory findings simply don't match the runner's racing history. Marathoner Don Kardong, not known for his sprint but highly regarded for his ability to hold a fast pace, had only 53% slow-twitch cells. But there's always a hedge: "his slow fibers were large," reported Dr. Costill, who helped coordinate the tests.

3. Parker, John L., "Olympic Forum," *Runner's World*, November, 1972.

4. Costill, David L., *A Scientific Approach to Distance Running*, Tafnews Press, 1979, p. 60.

5. Ibid., p. 32.

6. Daniels, Jack, et al., *Conditioning for Distance Runners*, John Wiley & Sons, N.Y., 1978, p. 13.

7. Ibid., p. 6.

8. Lydiard, Arthur and Gilmour, Garth, *Running the Lydiard Way*, World Publications, 1978, p. 16.

9. Daniels, p. 6.

10. Costill, p. 79.

11. Ibid., p. 18.

12. Daniels, p. 7.

13. Costill, p. 25.

14. Ibid., p. 11.

15. Ibid., p. 79.

16. See generally: Bale, John and Sang, Joe, *Kenyan Running*, Frank Cass & Co. Ltd., 1996; and Tanser, Toby, *Train Hard, Win Easy: The Kenyan Way*, Tafnews Press, 1997.

Chapter 12

1. Martin, David and Coe, Peter, *Training Distance Runners*, Human Kinetics, 1991, p. 69.

2. Parker, John L., *Running Times*, January, 1996.

Chapter 15

1. Martin and Coe, p. 154.

Chapter 16

1. See, for instance, Wilt, Fred, *How They Train Long Distances*, Tafnews Press, 1973.

2. Coe and Martin; Noakes, p. 154

3. Counsilman, James E., *Competitive Swimming Manual for Coaches and Swimmers*, Counsilman Co., Inc., Bloomington, IN, 1977.

4. Shermer, Michael, *Cycling Endurance and Speed*, Contemporary Books, 1987.

5. Costill and Wilmore, p. 84.

6. Noakes, p. 103.

7. Tinley, Scott, *Scott Tinley's Winning Triathlon*, Contemporary Books, Chicago, 1986; Allen, Mark, *Mark Allen's Total Triathlete*, Contemporary Books, 1988.

Chapter 17

1. Edwards, Sally. *Heart Zone Training*, Adams Media Corp., 1992.

2. Cooper, Kenneth H., *Aerobics*, Evans and Co., 1968.

Selected Bibliography

Allen, Mark, *Mark Allen's Total Triathlete*, Contemporary Books, Chicago, 1988.

Bale, John and Sang, Joe, *Kenyan Running*, Frank Cass & Co. Ltd., London, 1996.

Benson, Roy, *The Runner's Coach*, Cedarwinds, Tallahassee, 1995.

Brems, Marianne, *The Fit Swimmer*, Contemporary Books, Chicago, 1984.

Martin, David and Coe, Peter, *Training Distance Runners*, Human Kinetics, Champaign, IL, 1991.

Cooper, Kenneth H., *Aerobics*, Evans and Co., New York, 1968.

Costill, David L., *A Scientific Approach to Distance Running*, Tafnews Press, Los Altos, CA, 1979.

Counsilman, James E., *Competitive Swimming Manual for Coaches and Swimmers*, Counsilman Co., Inc., Bloomington, IN, 1977.

Daniels, Jack, et al., *Conditioning for Distance Runners*, John Wiley & Sons, N.Y., 1978.

Edwards, Sally, *The Heart Rate Monitor Book*, Polar Electro, Inc., NY, 1993.

Edwards, Sally, *Heart Zone Training*, Adams Media Corp., Holbrook, MA, 1992.

Edwards, Sally, *Triathlon: A Triple Fitness Sport*, Contemporary Books, Chicago, 1983.

Galloway, Jeff, *Galloway's Book on Running*, Shelter Publications, Inc., 1984.

Harris, Reg, *The Part-Time Runner*, P.T.R. Publications, Napa, CA, 1983.

Henderson, Joe, *Road Racers and Their Training*, Tafnews Press, Los Altos, CA, 1995.

Janssen, Petter G.J.M., *Training Lactate Pulse-Rate*, Polar Electro Oy, Finland, 1987.

Lydiard, Arthur and Gilmour, Garth, *Running the Lydiard Way*, World Publications, 1978.

Moore, Kenny, "Watching Their Steps," *Sports Illustrated*, May 3, 1973.

Noakes, Tim, *Lore of Running*, Human Kinetics, Champaign, IL, 1991.

Parker, John L. and Liquori, Marty, *Guide for the Elite Runner*, Seaview Books, NY, 1980.

Parker, John L., *Runners and Other Dreamers*, Cedarwinds, Tallahassee, 1989.

Shermer, Michael, *Cycling Endurance and Speed*, Contemporary Books, Chicago, 1987.

Sisson Mark, *Training and Racing Biathlons*, Primal Urge Press, Los Angeles, 1989.

Tanser, Toby, *Train Hard, Win Easy: The Kenyan Way*, Tafnews Press, Los Altos, CA, 1997.

Tinley, Scott, *Scott Tinley's Winning Triathlon*, Contemporary Books, Chicago, 1986.

Town, Glenn P. and Kearney, Todd, *Swim, Bike, Run*, Human Kinetics, Champaign, IL, 1994.

Town, Glenn P., *Science of Triathlon Training and Competition*, Human Kinetics, Champaign, IL, 1985.

Wilmore, Jack, and Costill, David. *Physiology of Sport and Exercise*, Human Kinetics, 1994.

Wiener, Harvey S., *Total Swimming*, Simon & Schuster, NY, 1980.

Wilt, Fred, *How They Train Long Distances*, Tafnews Press, Los Altos, CA, 1973.

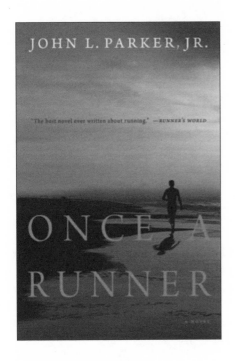

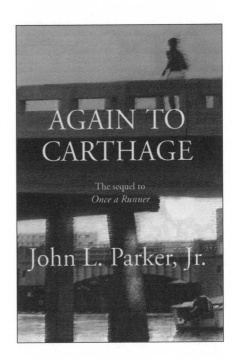